AF307616

Marx Abbott Hardy Machiavelli Chesterton Cooper Emerson Joyce Austen Hugo Defoe Melville Montaigne Haggard Grimm Eliot Stoker Carroll Christie Haggard Molière Schiller Wilde Maupassant Byron Engels Garnett Einstein Fitzgerald Hawthorne Smith Kafka Goethe Dostoyevsky Hall Cotton Kipling Doyle Willis Baum Henry Nietzsche Leslie Dumas Flaubert Turgenev Balzac Stockton Vatsyayana Crane Burroughs Verne Curtis Tocqueville Gogol Vinci Homer Widger Tolstoy Whitman Busch Darwin Thoreau Potter Freud Zola Lawrence Twain Scott Kant Jowett Stevenson Dickens Plato Harte Andersen Hesse London Descartes Burton Poe Aristotle Wells Voltaire Cervantes Hale James Hastings Cooke Bunner Shakespeare Irving Richter Chambers da Shaw Wodehouse Doré Dante Chekhov Benedict Alcott Swift Pushkin Newton

The Canadian Girl at Work A Book of Vocational Guidance

Marjory MacMurchy, Lady Willison

Imprint

This book is part of TREDITION CLASSICS

Author: Marjory MacMurchy, Lady Willison
Cover design: Buchgut, Berlin – Germany

Publisher: tredition GmbH, Hamburg - Germany
ISBN: 978-3-8472-1649-0

www.tredition.com
www.tredition.de

The

Canadian Girl at Work

A BOOK OF VOCATIONAL GUIDANCE

By

MARJORY MacMURCHY

Prepared at the Instance of the Minister of Education
for Use in Ontario School Libraries

Printed by Order of the Legislative Assembly of Ontario

TORONTO

Printed and Published by A. T. Wilgress, Printer to the King's Most
Excellent Majesty

1919

Copyright, Canada, 1919, by the
Minister of Education for Ontario

PREFACE

The object of *The Canadian Girl at Work* is to assist girls in finding satisfactory employment. The further aim of showing them what constitutes a right attitude toward work and toward life through work, underlies the account of each occupation. The book is meant for girls, and for the assistance of fathers and mothers, of teachers, and of those who are interested in questions of training and employment.

The life of the average woman is divided, generally, into two periods of work, that of paid employment and that of home-making. No adequate scheme of training for girls can fail to take account of this fact. They should be equipped with knowledge and skill for home-making, and assisted in making the best use of their years in paid work. Happily, it appears from an investigation of the conditions affecting girls as wage-earners that the knowledge which helps them to be good home-makers is necessary to their well-being in paid employment. Technical training and skill are not more helpful to a girl at work than specialized knowledge in matters of food, clothing, health, and daily regimen. Lack of training in home-making is probably the greatest drawback which a girl in paid employment can have. Her business during her first years of paid employment may not require much skill or experience, but her living conditions require all the specialized woman's knowledge that training can give her.

To bring about in the life of a girl a satisfactory connection between paid employment and home-making, and to show the home employments in their rightful place as occupations of the first importance, are necessary objectives in any book of this character.

When considering the employments of to-day as part of their own lives, girls of the twentieth century may well look back through the long ages to women's work in the past. [1] The study of anthropology appears to indicate that in primeval ages women began the textile industry and, possibly, agriculture. There seems to be no doubt that they were primitive architects, and that they tamed some of the smaller domestic animals. They had most to do with the preparation of food and may have introduced the use of herbs and medicines. They were spinners, weavers, upholsterers, and sail-makers. Most of these employments were taken up by men and specialized and developed almost past imagination. It is evident that women have always worked, and worked hard. If they had not done so, the race would not have reached its present position, and women themselves would have remained undeveloped, without a realization of their own possibilities.

The history of Anglo-Saxon times shows women engaged in spinning, weaving, dyeing, and embroidering, carrying on these industrial arts in the home, side by side with the work of the house. The work of women in home manufactures was a by-industry, not occupying the worker's whole time, but nevertheless an important occupation. Later, women were employed in many kinds of industrial work as assistants to their husbands and fathers. It is doubtful if wages were paid for such work. Employment of this kind is not to be thought of merely as a romantic or picturesque accompaniment of home life. Houses and comforts centuries back were not such as they are to-day; and the work of women was toil, side by side with men who toiled also.

The modern factory did not originate industrial work. The factory carried many industries away from the home where they had originated; and women followed their work to large establishments where they were trained to work collectively. The statement can be made with truth that machinery has made it possible for women to perform work for which their strength would otherwise have been insufficient. Through the industrial revolution brought about by factory work, the general body of women workers became wage-earners, rather than unpaid workers who contributed to the financial earnings of their fathers and husbands.

In Canada, the process of development of women's work in the past fifty years has been rapid. The grandmothers of the women of this generation carded wool and used spinning wheels within the memory of workers of less than middle age. One old woman who died not many years ago told how she used to bake in an oven out-of-doors and had dyed homespun with butternut. The soap cauldron stood on the levelled stump of what had been once a forest tree. Candles were moulded in iron moulds. Household industries were carried on expertly in the homes of pioneers by the women of the family.

When these days had gone, there followed other days in which the children of the pioneers devoted themselves to the schooling so highly esteemed but rarely enjoyed by their parents. The boys, after school life, turned to business, railway employments, teaching, banking, farming, became ministers, lawyers, doctors, or gave their thoughts to politics. The girls taught school, were milliners or dressmakers, went into shops, or became the wives of nation builders in every walk of life. A few were nurses, journalists, doctors, or missionaries.

The work of that generation has been followed by a century in which Canadian girls are invited to share in nearly every form of activity. This great freedom with its many opportunities has come for noble ends. What the girls of to-day must strive to do is to take up their work with a vision of what it may be made to mean—men and women in co-partnership laying the foundations of a new earth.

It is probable that the social and domestic conditions of the earliest workers were far below those of the average worker of to-day. But, although present conditions are better than those of the past, the process of amelioration should be greatly advanced by this generation. The increasing opportunities of girls, both in home-making and paid employment, are likely to become a contributing factor in the humanizing of every form of industry. We have learned to realize the possibilities of machinery. What we must do now is to imagine and realize the possibilities of the individual worker. This can be done only through study, experience, and actual work in industrial occupations which offer employment to women.

The woman of the home has work of unrivalled value. She has to study new standards of living, to help to control the food supply, to improve the health of children, and to lower the rate of infant mortality. A standard of living in each community might be tabulated by women home-makers. Such information should be available in each locality and should be accessible to all classes in the community. How are workers—girls, boys, men, or women—to know on what sums individuals and families can live and maintain health and efficiency in one district or another, if these matters are not studied, determined, and published for their use?

THE CANADIAN GIRL AT WORK

CHAPTER I

THINKING ABOUT WORK

Thinking about work is the beginning of one of the happiest and most useful of our experiences. Through work there comes to us the pleasure of a growing knowledge of the great world and its wonders, the delight of intercourse with other people, and the happiness of friendship with our fellow-workers. Work well done is a doorway to whatever good things we most desire. Best of all, perhaps, to the girl who is earning her living, is the satisfaction of feeling that she is a useful citizen, doing her part in the development of Canada.

Canadian girls have a wide field from which to choose their particular form of occupation. To choose wisely is a duty we owe to ourselves and to our country—to ourselves, because a wise choice helps to secure our happiness in work; to our country, because she has a right to the best we can offer her in return for the peace and freedom in which we live under her laws.

Every year new varieties of employment and new positions in old employments are being added to the field of work for girls and women. Work at home is being systematized, and new devices are increasing the efficiency of the work of a home. Among the girls who are beginning work to-day are some who will develop further the management of the home on modern economic and social lines. Forward-thinking people anticipate a great advance which will be made by the girls of the twentieth century in the management of homes.

But what of the workers outside the home? Opportunities of employment are steadily increasing. Already women are making a business of growing vegetables and flowers, are engaged in the work of poultry farms, bee-keeping, and in dairy production. Women are undertaking the work of chemical experts in factories. Girls are driving motors and collecting waste. They are shopping experts, employment experts, house furnishers, agents for renting houses, and one woman has become an expert in testing flour for a great milling industry. These are new employments. Hundreds of thousands of girls and women are at work in the long-established women's employments, as factory workers, saleswomen, stenographers, house workers, telephone and telegraph operators, waitresses, milliners, dressmakers and seamstresses, teachers, and nurses.

Some opportunities for employment are close at hand; others are farther away. Sometimes it is best to begin with the nearest work. But in any case the girl should take time to think of her employment. There are various helpers to whom she may turn when she is beginning to think about work—her father and mother, her teachers, the Government Employment Bureau, a good private employment expert such as may be found in the Young Women's Christian Association, or an older friend who is able to advise her and, finally, the girl should help herself. She should think carefully of the kind of work it seems likely that she may get to do and ask herself what employment she finds most attractive and whether she has some aptitude for it.

The following are some of the questions a girl should ask herself when she is thinking of her employment: Shall I be able to improve and become more skilful in my work? Will the work give me good companionship? Are the surroundings clean and comfortable, and will they be good for my health and the health of other workers? Is the employment likely to give me a fair wage?

The statements made about wages in different employments apply generally to the scale of wages paid in one particular city. No one set of figures can be given which will state accurately the wages in many cities and towns and country districts. The value of wages cannot be estimated properly by the girl unless she knows at the same time what her living expenses are to be. She must know, too, the standard of efficiency required in the employment. These questions are discussed specially in Chapters XXIII and XXIV. When the girl reads any statement concerning wages, she should remember that the figures given represent only an approximate estimate. That is, while these wages have actually been paid in one place, the same wages will not be offered in these employments in every part of the country. Generally speaking, the figures quoted represent mid-war wages.

The most important fact for the girl to learn about employment is that when she does well-chosen work in the right spirit, she will find in it happiness and usefulness. Through her work she will learn what an interesting place the world is, and because she is a worker she will be the companion of great workers who are advancing civilization every day. She may feel sure that there is work for her to do, that she will find work good, and the world a friendly place.

CHAPTER II

THE GIRL WHO WORKS IN A FACTORY

A girl's first impression of a factory is likely to be that it is a busy place. The people at work and the work itself will seem strange to her. She may even feel that she will never get used to her new surroundings. But she should not allow herself to be discouraged. Although she may have forgotten her first day in school when she was a little girl of five or six, no doubt the schoolroom seemed to her then a very strange place, but how quickly it became familiar and homelike.

The girl will enter the factory as a learner. Her wages will not be high, but she will be paid for her first week, although it is hardly likely that her work at first will be worth the money she receives for it. One of the more experienced factory employees will be given the task of training her. So the girl beginning work in a factory is really learning as she did at school although now she is getting wages. The factory finds it worth while to train beginners, and it does so in the hope that they will become capable operators who will be in their places regularly.

One of the most important truths for the girl in the factory to realize is that the more there is to learn about her work the better her future will be as a worker. If there is so little to learn that she needs only a few days to become independent of any training, then she will be sure to find unskilled girls and low wages in this place of employment. She should not be satisfied permanently with such work. The best positions are for skilled employees and, therefore, every girl ought to become a skilled worker. To be a skilled worker means that you can command good wages and that you are more certain of steady employment than an unskilled employee, since your employer will wish to retain your services even when the work in the factory is slack. The girl, therefore, should not be anxious to find that there is little to learn about her work. When she discovers that it will be some time before she can carry on all the operations required, then she may be sure that she is learning an employment which will be of value to her. It is exactly the same as in school. No one was ever so clever as to be able to learn to read in one day, yet we all know how well worth while it is to be able to read.

How is the girl to choose the industry in which she hopes to find work? [2] She should make inquiries about a factory before she enters it. She may have a friend who is working in a whitewear factory, or a biscuit factory, or who is making boxes. The friend probably will be willing to speak to the foreman or forewoman about the girl's employment. But she should notice the surroundings in which she means to work. Is the workroom light and airy? Are the conditions under which she must work sanitary? Are the workers respectable and well-behaved? If she is to work where there is machinery, it should be properly guarded, so that she will not be in danger. She should not choose a factory where the hours are longer than the average nor one where over-time is encouraged. The management also should be fair and considerate.

The kind of work carried on in the factory should give her an opportunity to become a skilled worker. If the girls employed are all young girls earning only a low wage, and there is little chance of promotion, then, while it may be convenient for her to begin in such a factory, she should not be content to stay there. She must be sure to make herself a skilled worker, with a good chance of promotion and a fair certainty of receiving a higher wage than is usually paid to a beginner.

When the girl knows the kind of factory for which she ought to look, she may very well ask herself what qualifications she should possess in order to become a successful factory worker. She should be healthy, of good average physical strength, quick in her movements, with some natural mechanical ability, good eyesight, and quick, steady hands. If she is to begin where there is power machinery, it is an advantage to have had some practice in running power machinery. Such practice she can get at a trade or a technical school, most of which have night classes. Otherwise there is not very much that a girl can learn about the actual work of a factory before she enters it. She must make up her mind, however, to learn when once she is in the factory. She should learn as many different operations as possible. Nothing so increases the value of a worker as to be able to fill a number of different positions. She should try to understand as much of the business of the establishment as possible. Then she will find herself taking a keen interest in the work and she will be better able to enjoy her own part in it.

The girl's first wage in a factory is not likely to be large enough to cover all her expenses. But, when she is a skilled worker, her wage should provide her with reasonable necessaries and comfort and leave a margin for saving, emergencies, and improvement. Every worker should realize that good conditions are an important part of what one gets for one's work. It is advisable to be satisfied with a little less money in an establishment where opportunity is given for promotion, the guarding of health, and recreation, and where the surroundings are clean and attractive, sometimes even delightful, rather than to get a little more money, and be driven beyond one's strength, or compelled to spend a great part of the day in unpleasant surroundings. Lunch and rest rooms, a separate locker for her clothes, books to read, an open tennis court or other opportunity for play, are greatly valued by the girl at work, as they constitute, in reality, a bonus in addition to her wages.

As soon as she is experienced, the girl in the factory is almost certain to find herself on "piece-work." That is, instead of being paid a daily or weekly wage, she will receive a set price for each article or "piece" completed.

Speed in piece-work as a rule is a means by which she can earn high wages. The wages of a beginner in a city may be eight or nine dollars a week; wages vary, however, according to the locality and the character of the work. The wages paid to experienced operators vary in a number of cases from fifteen to twenty dollars a week. Exceptional workers who have special ability earn more. With regard to piece-work, the girl should have sufficient judgment not to force herself beyond her strength. She may lose her health by a few years' overwork and become unable to support herself. The speed of the worker is a subject for careful study both by the girl and her employer. The girl will find that she can maintain high speed for a certain length of time only and that her output actually will be greater, week in and week out, if she slackens when she begins to feel a strain.

The most successful girl will not change about readily from one place to another. If a girl is certain that she can improve her work and her position, and if she has come to a careful decision, feeling sure that her present conditions are not what they might be, then she will be wise to change her place of employment. But the young girl who changes every few weeks or months is in danger of spoiling not only her prospects as a paid worker, but her whole life. While this danger is found in other employments, it is perhaps greatest in the case of the factory worker.

"Some of the finest people I know," said a well-known factory owner not long ago, "are at work in our factories." This may be said as truly all over the country. It applies equally to men and women workers. Generous, unselfish, efficient women and girls, as are many of these workers, are a source of strength to their families and the country. They are using their lives wisely and well, whether they continue as paid workers or leave the factory to take charge of the care of a home.

CHAPTER III

THE SALESWOMAN

The employment department of a big store is the testing place through which many girls who mean to be saleswomen must pass before they reach the store itself. Naturally the girl should be careful to do herself justice when she goes to the employment department. The head of the department will be certain to note her appearance carefully. The girl should make sure that she is cleanly and neatly dressed; she should speak quietly and politely; and she should show that sincere willingness to be cheerful, obliging, and agreeable which she will find one of the best aids in her life both at work and at home. To enter a store no particular training is required. The girl leaving school when she is fourteen, fifteen, or sixteen, who is able to read and write correctly and who has a thorough knowledge of the common rules of arithmetic can hope to obtain a position in a store.

Having once obtained a position in a large store, the girl will find herself part of an establishment where perhaps hundreds or thousands of people are employed. It is probable that her position will be an easy one suited to her age, without much responsibility, and with small pay, but, if she shows interest and willingness to learn, she will be in line for promotion. There are many positions which carry with them great responsibility, and correspondingly large wages. A girl's chance to occupy some day such a position depends largely on herself. She should try to understand as much as possible about the store and its methods and rules, and she should make her work part of the successful work of the establishment.

In a large store the younger girls are employed as messenger girls, parcel girls, markers, or, after some time in a store, a younger girl may help in the care of the stock. The payment received in these positions is small. Indeed, the problem of the youngest girls in the store is not an easy one. The girl herself should try to realize that this big store in which she is employed must be to her what the high school or college is to other girls who stayed at school when she went to work. Here, in the store, she should continue her education, which is to take the practical form of a business training.

Unfortunately, some of the girls thus employed are indifferent to their work. These are the inattentive, listless girls who look about them idly, instead of attending to the needs of possible customers, or who spend more than half the time talking to their friends visiting the store or to their fellow-workers. One large establishment reports that only one third of their staff become skilled in salesmanship. Another famous firm of employers says that twenty-five per cent. of their girls do not improve, another twenty-five per cent. are only fairly satisfactory, while fifty per cent. are satisfactory. The girl who enters the employment of a store should determine to become a skilled saleswoman.

Fortunately, the work of the saleswoman is steadily rising in its standing as a good occupation. It is becoming skilled employment. Already there are a number of schools which teach salesmanship, and many of the larger departmental stores have courses of instruction for their salespeople. The managers of these stores say that this training pays both the store and its staff of employees. After training the employees make better wages and the store earns a higher percentage. Any girl who wants to be a saleswoman should, if possible, take a course in salesmanship either at a business college, a trade school, or at a Young Women's Christian Association, or she should try to find a position in a store where there is a school for employees.

Our young saleswoman will study her store, she will take lessons in salesmanship, she will be interested in her work and eager to learn. Such a girl will find that the place of her employment is a world in miniature, where she can study life and human nature and where she may become a useful and well-equipped member of society. No girl who is a good saleswoman can fail to learn how to deal with many different kinds of people and to have many opportunities of making friends among her fellow-workers.

It is not difficult for the average girl to become an efficient saleswoman. To recapitulate—she should be neat and pleasing in appearance, quick to learn, willing to obey, with good manners and bright intelligence, and she should be interested in her work. She should have a "head for figures," a knowledge of correct English, and ability to work quickly and courteously at the same time. She should, of course, have a thorough knowledge of the commodity she is selling. The more accurate her knowledge of materials, the better saleswoman she will make. She should also take a personal interest in the wants of her customers. Her object is to sell articles which will give satisfaction.

The average earnings of saleswomen at times seem disappointingly small. It should be remembered, however, that the indifferent or careless girl lowers the average. The successful saleswoman, after some years of work, may earn from fifteen to twenty dollars a week. A great many girls earn less. The beginner may get five or six dollars a week or, if she is in an establishment which pays no employee less than a certain amount, she may get seven or eight dollars. The girl who earns less than eight dollars a week after a year or two years is not a successful saleswoman and is not likely to be kept on in any well-managed store. The saleswoman who is dissatisfied with her wage may ask at any time to have reference made to her actual sales, of which an account is kept. Wages are based on sales. Sometimes a commission is paid on sales over a certain amount. In any case, the girl feels that there is a direct connection between her successful salesmanship and her wages. Character, skill, tact, and energy are all required for successful salesmanship. The saleswoman who really gives herself to the work of serving and satisfying her customers finds her employment an exacting one.

A saleswoman may be promoted to have charge of stock; she may become assistant buyer or head of a department; and in somewhat rare cases she may become a buyer. These are all responsible positions requiring unusual business ability and character. The salaries are high. If a saleswoman has excellent business ability, she may, after years of experience, become an important influence in the management of the store. Some departments offer greater opportunities than others. The more expensive the article to be sold, the more is required from the saleswoman. A very young girl will not be found selling coats and cloaks or expensive suits and dresses. "The customer who is spending a large amount of money wants to have confidence in the judgment of the saleswoman," is the saying of an expert in store management.

The large department store, while it affords training and opportunity to the girl who intends to become a competent saleswoman, employs many girls and women in occupations other than salesmanship. In the store there is a large clerical staff, including stenographers, who may receive promotion to the position of private secretaries and bookkeepers. Telephone and telegraph operators are among the employees. The store shoppers act in connection with mail orders and orders received by telephone. The advertising department employs writers, artists, proof-readers, and card and sign writers. Milliners are employed in the millinery department and fitters and dressmakers in the alteration departments. Manicurists and hair-dressers carry on their special occupations, and waitresses are employed in the store lunchroom or restaurant. Trained nurses have positions in the store hospital and visit employees in their homes. Machine and handworkers carry out special orders in making curtains, cushions, lampshades, etc. A store school employs teachers of salesmanship and store system.

Many girls are employed as saleswomen in smaller stores which need only a few employees. The system of the great store is not so necessary in a small establishment, yet the individual saleswoman in the small store holds a responsible position. Sometimes a girl with business ability becomes in time assistant manager, or even part owner, of such a store. Ideas and initiative will tell wherever they are found, and the girl who is really interested in salesmanship will succeed in a large store or in a small one.

The hours are fairly long, sometimes longer than the average in women's occupations, but they are no longer than the hours required in many professional and other employments in which women are engaged.

The well-advised saleswoman will have interests outside of her work. She should study some interesting branch of knowledge and cultivate a hobby. She will find both pleasure and benefit in belonging to a club or other association. One of the most interesting developments in the large business establishment where numbers of men and women are employed is the organization for comradeship and improvement. Thrift is encouraged; opportunities are provided for exercise; sometimes those on the staff of such an establishment are offered housing of an attractive kind at moderate prices. The girls of the establishment may be provided with a club house.

Altogether, the character of this employment is complex and interesting. It is an attractive occupation, in which the girl is brought into relationship with people with whom she can help to develop a sociable, co-operative life, tending to improve her own character and usefulness and that of others.

CHAPTER IV

THE GIRL AT WORK IN AN OFFICE

The girl who hopes to succeed in office work should be able to spell correctly and should have a good general English education. It is true that some girls have taught themselves to spell correctly after they have entered business offices; and ambitious, sensible girls, who find that letters dictated to them contain words the meaning of which they do not know, study until their vocabularies are greatly enlarged and improved. But, while they are learning, the employer is not receiving the service to which he is entitled.

The only practical way for the average girl to enter a business office is by studying stenography. But to have a really satisfactory school training, the girl who means to be a stenographer should be ready to pass the entrance examination into a college or university. Three or four years' attendance at a high or secondary school is a necessary preparation for first-class office work. The girl who is a college graduate is not too well equipped to be a stenographer. Even if a girl is compelled, by the necessity of earning her living, to begin office work early, still she can, by determination, courage, and hard work, equip herself with a good business education. But it is only the exceptional girl who can do this. The girl who wishes to engage in office work should have three years, if possible, in a good secondary school, before she enters a business college.

The business college should be chosen carefully, and the girl in training should attend the classes for nine months or a year. This is the least time required for satisfactory training. Unfortunately, too many students take only six months, or even three, at a business school. The result is that they begin work only partly equipped with training for the office. Many employers complain that stenographers are incompetent and careless. One reason for this is that they have not had sufficient training; their stenography, typewriting, and other instruction have been only half mastered. Office work would be a better employment for girls if these half-trained and incompetent workers were not lowering wages, irritating employers, and limiting the work and responsibility with which girls would be entrusted if the average stenographer knew her work thoroughly.

The girl who leaves a business college to enter an office should not feel that there is nothing more to learn. No one can be a thoroughly competent stenographer until she has been a year at work in an office. The school teaches her how to handle her working tools.

But the real problems of office work are solved only in the office. There are endless details to be mastered. Every office has its own rules and customs and its own methods. It is necessary to learn how to meet people and deal with them. The girl must study the people with whom she works. She must learn how her employer likes to have his work done. The best workers keep on learning year by year.

Many of the qualities which go to make the ideal home-maker belong to the ideal worker in an office. The business girl will need self-control and tact. Her manners should be quiet and agreeable. An office is a place for work; and part of the usefulness of a business girl is in helping to make it a good place in which to work. She should therefore understand order and method. She should be tranquil and well poised. She should get her work done quickly without seeming to be in a hurry. Such a girl is a treasure in an office.

The business girl should be dressed suitably for her occupation. One of the first lessons for her to learn is that no employer is likely to believe that she can do good work if her general appearance is careless or untidy. Her dress should be quiet and pleasing, and it should not distract her attention from her work. A workmanlike dress can be very attractive. Business girls as a rule show taste and judgment in choosing their clothes and in keeping every detail of their appearance neat, suitable, and pleasing. Thrift in the matter of dressing and a suitable appearance are necessary factors in the success of a business girl's work.

The business girl must be trustworthy. She cannot be a success if her employer is in doubt as to whether she may talk about office business outside. Her memory should be good. It is a great help to have someone at hand who can remember a business conversation, where to find documents, addresses, and other memoranda. The girl will find that it is unsatisfactory to spend much time in social conversation. If she wishes to earn and keep the good opinion of her fellow-workers and her employer, she will attend to work, with only an occasional remark on anything not connected with office affairs.

The salaries earned by business girls vary greatly. There are girls at work in offices who are paid as little as five, six, or seven dollars a week. But these girls are very young, they are badly trained, unable to do good work of any kind, and they should hardly be called stenographers. They can address envelopes, do a little typewriting, answer the telephone, and so on. The well-equipped office girl should realize that she must keep up the standard of her employment, as one which needs thorough training and competent, well paid workers, so the work of the girl in business may remain a highly-respected and desirable occupation.

The supply of first-class office workers is never sufficient to meet the demand. A common wage for younger competent stenographers who have had some experience is twelve dollars. Experienced stenographers may get fifteen, eighteen, twenty, or twenty-five dollars, according to the positions they occupy, the character of the work, and the responsibility involved. Girls with managing ability may be promoted to hold important positions. They may become assistant managers of offices or confidential clerks or secretaries. Women in these positions receive salaries of from two to three thousand dollars a year. In an exceptional case a woman who is a manager may receive four or five thousand. But such positions and such women workers are rare indeed. Eighteen dollars a week is regarded as a good salary for a capable stenographer of some years' experience. The average stenographer receives as a rule two weeks' holidays with wages. This is an important consideration for it helps to secure her health and general well-being.

It is often said that a small office offers the best opportunity for a clever girl to win promotion. She is given work of all kinds to do and can make herself indispensable to her employer. On the other hand, the work may be easier in a large office since it is organized on well-established lines. Salaries, generally speaking, are higher in large offices, but there are fewer opportunities for promotion.

An unusually competent office girl with some capital may become a public stenographer. But, in order to succeed, she must have business ability and should understand clearly what she can afford and what she cannot afford in office equipment, rent, and so on. The work of a public stenographer is very exacting. Many stenographers are employed in the service of the Government. In general, an examination is required for a position in the civil service. The work and hours are regular and not exacting, and the pay is good. Many girls, however, find work in a business office more interesting, and opportunities for promotion are also better.

Some girls who have not the ability to become expert stenographers, may be exceptionally good typists. Such girls may find employment in typing letters from phonographs or dictaphones. Work with multigraphs, adding-machines, or comptometers is required in larger offices. Special positions may be obtained by girls who are of a mechanical turn or who have considerable manual dexterity. The girl who devotes herself to bookkeeping, if she has special ability, may occupy an important business position.

In whatever capacity she may be employed, the earnest and competent office-worker will find herself highly valued and well paid for her share of responsibility in the world of financial and commercial development.

CHAPTER V

LEARNING AFTER THE POSITION IS FOUND

The first few days, sometimes even the first few weeks, are often a little difficult for the girl who has found a position and goes to work for the first time. But she can take with her a few simple resolutions which will make most of her difficulties disappear and which may even change them into helps rather than hindrances. She can remember that all the responsible people she knows have had these same difficulties and have overcome them. This thought will encourage her to believe that what others have done she can do also. There is much that she may gain from this new position. It is like an open door whereby she may enter a new world.

The girl who is in her first position will find that she must adjust herself to conditions very different from those of home and school life. At home all her personal concerns have been of supreme importance, and she has been the object of unceasing love and care. At school her best interests have still been consulted, and she has been taught how both to work and play. She now begins to give back value for the care which has been taken of her at home and the teaching which she has received at school. After she is able to work for herself, it is really no one else's duty to support her. She cannot expect that busy people in the office or workroom will stop to listen to her. If she is feeling dull or discouraged, or if something has gone wrong in her private affairs, these things have nothing to do with her fellow-workers. They also have their private affairs. Therefore she must learn to be cheerful, not to talk about her own troubles, and to be, in brief, a grown-up, sensible, considerate person.

Two illustrations may help the girl to understand this difference between life in paid employment and school days or life at home. A girl once was offered a position in a large establishment by the man who was the head of the business. She had certain training and gifts which made him believe that she could do good work in his business. After her appointment she found that she was under the direction of the manager's chief of staff, who, as she soon discovered, had wanted someone else. She began to think out the position in which she found herself. "It is quite plain," she said to herself, "that the chief is a more important person than I am. He is not going to lose his position because he does not like me. It would not be just or right or good business if he did. The truth is that if I do not get on with him and convince him that I can do good work I am going to be a failure. It is part of my business to get on with the chief of staff." She had made the important discovery that it is wise to put oneself in the background and to work harmoniously with one's associates. After a year's hard work she had the satisfaction of being told by her chief, that, notwithstanding his early dissatisfaction with her appointment, she had won his approval, for she had convinced him of her efficiency.

The other illustration can be given in a few words, but it teaches a truth about paid employment which many girls need to learn. One day a woman called to see an important public man on a matter of business. When she came he was dictating a letter. He saw his caller as soon as he had finished. Before the conversation had well begun, his secretary came to the door and asked him to what address he wished the letter sent. When the secretary had gone out again, the man looked at his visitor and said laughing, yet with an expression of annoyance, "I cannot teach my secretary that it is her work to

look up addresses. She is here to save me trouble. I am not here to
save her trouble. But I cannot get her to understand that." The girl in
question was behaving in her work as if she had been a spoiled
child at home. It is to be hoped that she would have been ashamed
to ask her mother, for instance, to tell her an address which she
could look up for herself. Yet this girl was being paid to find addresses as part of her work.

The girl who is beginning paid employment will have to learn
largely from others how her work ought to be done, but she must
learn to depend on her own observation. Questions must be asked
occasionally, but it is unwise to ask too many. Ask information only
from those who are willing to answer. Everyone in the world of
work is busy as a rule, and comparatively few people will stop their
work to explain to someone else how a task ought to be done. There
are two classes of workers—those who require direction always,
and those who are able and willing to take responsibility. The girl at
first begins under direction but, as soon as she is familiar with what
she has to do and understands a good deal of the purpose of her
work, she should try, if possible, to develop responsibility. It is a
good plan to study how other people do their work. There is sure to
be someone among one's fellow-employees who is a specially good
worker. Study the methods and character of this worker and learn
from your observation how to do your own work. The girl in a new
position should resolutely avoid association with lazy, indifferent,
and idle fellow-employees. One of the first lessons for her to learn,
and sometimes one of the hardest, is that her time is not her own. It
belongs to her employer, who is paying for her work. Therefore her
own social engagements have no claim on her working hours.

It is apparent that certain qualifications and characteristics ensure
success in paid work—good temper, self-control, common sense,
kindness, and a sense of what is fair are of inestimable value to the
girl worker. Moreover, she must be in earnest in her determination
to find work and keep it. She should have some secondary employment at which she can work if her regular employment is slack.
And through all the changes and difficulties of her working life, a
girl should know how to keep well, for health is a great asset.

She should add to these essentials a feeling of responsibility and a desire to understand the problems of management in the business in which she is employed. In addition, let her have that sense of honour which will keep her from a betrayal of confidential information. The loyal worker is always valued and respected.

CHAPTER VI

WHAT EVERY GIRL NEEDS TO KNOW

The world the girl has to live in is the everyday world we know. Some people say that the world is commonplace, and so it is if we look at it from one point of view. But the truth is that the commonplace and the wonderful are so closely joined together that it is impossible to separate them. The girl needs commonplace gifts to live in the world, or she will not prosper. She needs also to be able to see and understand the wonderful side of life. To appreciate both the commonplace and the wonderful should be part of her endeavour. A great deal depends on her training. What shall we choose for her? She may work at home or in paid employment, but she needs certain training, because she is a girl, just as a soldier needs training, because he is a soldier.

First, the girl ought to know how to keep well. Good health is a precious possession, and we may have a great deal to do with whether we are strong and healthy or weak and half-ill most of the time. If the girl is to be a home-maker, she needs good health. What a sad place a home is if the home-maker is a constant sufferer! If the girl is in a shop, a factory, an office, a telephone exchange, a school, or a hospital, unless she is a reasonably healthy girl her success in her work is greatly lessened, if indeed it is possible for her to succeed at all. If she is an actress or an artist, she undergoes a constant strain on her nervous energy. Artists and actresses need good health, possibly more so even than the average woman in paid employment. So, no matter what the girl is to do, she should be healthy.

But she requires certain definite kinds of knowledge, so that she may know how to keep well. The first is knowing what to eat. There is scarcely anything that interferes more with the health and success of the girl worker than ignorance of what is nutritious food. A woman who is very fond of girls who work and who knows hundreds of them, said once that she would like to give every girl she knew this knowledge about food. There is no way of acquiring it except by learning. Our ideal girl will learn food values and how food should be prepared. Every girl in the world, no matter who she is, is better off for this knowledge. It is part of the foundation of good health. The girl in business requires a special warning to be sure that her luncheon gives her sufficient nourishment for her work.

In order to be healthy, girls must know, also, how to dress. This should include some knowledge of the making of clothing, how to cut out, and how to sew, and also some skill in mending and re-modelling. Looking into the future for the well-being of our ideal girl, we see that her appearance as well as her health depends not a little on her skill as a wise buyer and maker of clothing. Her early income as a worker is not likely to be large. It may be very small. It will need all her skill to make the best use of this income.

In order to acquire skill in the management of food and clothing and so ensure her health, a girl must understand the management of money. Some day she will have the spending of an income. Either she will earn the income in paid employment, or it will be part of her work as a home-maker to manage the spending of the house money. Now, money cannot be spent wisely except by planning. The girl should learn how to divide her income, to allot so much for food, so much for clothing, so much for shelter, so much for im-provement, recreation, and holidays, so much for the dentist and the doctor, so much to be saved, so much for religious obligations and benevolence, and for safety a margin over, because there are always unforeseen calls on one's income. This planning for the proper division of her income may sound at first a little bewilder-ing. But after all, what is it but learning what we can afford to spend? We begin by buying a little carefully, and as we go on we acquire knowledge and skill. Few things which the twentieth centu-ry girl can learn will stand her in better stead in everyday life, or help her more constantly, than knowing how to spend her income wisely, honestly, and helpfully.

We have spoken at some length about food and clothing as they affect health. Quite as important to health are rest and recreation. A girl needs not only plenty of refreshing sleep, but play also and what most people call "good times." It is a mistake to suppose that we can be healthy without play. Often when we are out of sorts, sad, depressed, and gloomy, and our friends are sorry for us and think something dreadful must have happened to make us so unhappy, all that we need in reality is sleep, fresh air, exercise, and play. It is not being a heroine to be sad. Most real heroines are happy people. There is nothing heroic in making other people depressed by our gloomy faces. The ideal girl is healthy and happy, she sleeps eight hours or more at night, and plays a reasonable part of her time. To play all the time is very dull, even more dull than to work all the time. But each day, if possible, one should have some happy play time.

Then, too, the ideal girl will try to see that she helps others to be as healthy and happy as she is herself. Part of the value of knowing how to keep well is that it teaches us how to keep other people well. We should know how others should be fed and clothed and cared for. The girl of the twentieth century needs some knowledge of nursing. It is not necessary for her to be a trained nurse, but she should have some of the knowledge and skill of the trained nurse.

Among the things that every girl needs to know is something of the importance of friendship. The best gifts in the world are love, kindness, faithfulness, sincerity, and purity. It is through our relations with other human beings and our love for them that we begin to understand the love of God.

CHAPTER VII

THE HOUSE WORKER — DOMESTIC SCIENCE

A young woman who is now the author of two successful novels earned the money she needed to attend a teachers' training school by working as a domestic servant. It was the quickest and most convenient way for her to earn a certain sum of money. Her decision and independence of character kept her from hesitating for a moment to make use of this employment. One young woman who is a capable real estate agent takes a position as an experienced general servant when her usual business is slack. A woman at the head of a large business, which she originated and developed herself, earned her living as a domestic until she was twenty-five years old. There is no reason why any of us should be kept from doing good domestic work if it is the most suitable and convenient employment for us.

The disadvantages of domestic work, as it is generally arranged at present, are that the house worker is required to live away from home; her own special sleeping and living accommodation is sometimes not of the best; she has comparatively little time that is absolutely her own; she feels that she is placed at a social disadvantage as compared with other girls who are her friends and who are earning a living in other paid work, and she may be lonely, as a consequence of being often the only paid worker in the household. These are facts to be considered. But it is possible that a re-arrangement of household work, undertaken by modern employers and clever modern girls, who have a gift for household management, as well as character and initiative, may provide a solution for these disadvantages.

The advantages of domestic work include good wages, and more comfortable living conditions than the average paid worker can secure for herself. The house worker has also variety in work, freedom to move about at her work, and freedom from the rigid rules necessary in big business establishments. She is afforded an opportunity to become a highly skilled worker, and she can find a permanent position if she is competent and wishes to remain in one place. Above all, the house worker is getting the best training for home-making.

The wages of the house worker include board, lodging, and washing, and often some part at least of her working clothes. She has two weeks' holidays with wages. She may save in a year a quarter or a third as much money as the entire earnings of her girl friends. At twelve dollars a week, working forty-two weeks in the year, the girl in a factory can earn five hundred and four dollars, out of which she has of course to pay all her expenses. The house worker who is earning twenty-five, thirty or thirty-five dollars a month can easily save two hundred dollars in a year, and a number of them do so. Girls in other paid employments, who pay board and lodging, washing, and carfare out of ten or twelve dollars a week, are practically unable to save anything.

A competent house worker is beyond the fear of unemployment, while the possibility of unemployment or of being laid off for a number of weeks is an anxiety to many other paid women workers. When she marries and has a home of her own to take care of, the house worker is at a great advantage. She can take up the work of a home easily, and her management is a success from the beginning.

The accomplishment most frequently required from the domestic worker is ability to cook. The girl who has a natural gift in this direction should take pains to develop it. She may have to begin to earn her living when she is quite young. In this case she should apply for a position as second maid in a household where a cook is kept, and she should be careful to learn from the cook all that she needs to know in order to become a professional expert in cooking. Or she should look for a position as house worker with an employer who is herself a good housekeeper and who is willing to train her.

The improvement of housework conditions is largely in the hands of household employees. If a young woman is an excellent cook and a competent household manager, she can make practically her own conditions with women employers. If she prefers to live at home or in a room of her own outside the house where she is employed, she can explain to her employer the hours that she is willing to be on duty and how the work of the house can be arranged so that she can accomplish the greater part of it during these hours. She will be certain to find some intelligent woman employer who will agree to her conditions. Only the first-class worker, who can plan and carry out her plans successfully, will be able to do this; and every woman employer may not see the benefit of such an arrangement. There are a number of households where the woman in charge will be glad to accept service during half the day, but here also the house worker must be first class. The trained domestic worker of high qualifications, able to do her work to perfection, and to consider intelligently how the work of the household can be organized, will add greatly to the standing of this employment.

The house worker should have a fairly good general education. The better her general education, the more successful she is likely to be. She should be intelligent, obliging, and adaptable. She should have a strong sense of honour, for she is largely on her own responsibility, and the welfare of the home is often trusted in her hands. The ideal household employee should have some of the qualities of the artist. The work of a fine cook is artistic, and the perfect care of a house requires both the eye and the hand of an artist. No woman can be a success as a paid house worker who is not kind. She often has some part of the care of children, and it is wrong to have an ill-tempered or unkind person in charge of, or in company with, children. Besides this, the care of a house, the cooking of food, cleanliness, and the work of adapting oneself to the wants of others cannot be carried out well and cheerfully unless the worker responsible for this work is kind.

Wages are unusually good in domestic work as compared with other employments for women. Some girls, however, are underpaid. A girl may receive, for instance, twelve dollars a month. No girl with initiative or knowledge of housework needs to remain in such a position. Wages vary from twenty, twenty-two, to twenty-five, thirty, and thirty-five dollars, according to the locality, the nature of the work, and the skill of the worker. A first-class cook commands high wages. So also does a first-class managing housekeeper. A general servant of ability and character, who undertakes most of the work of a household, with the exception of the washing, will receive twenty, twenty-five or thirty dollars. In some parts of the country her wages may be higher. If trained workers, who have special gifts for household management and who feel that they can do better in this employment than any other, would undertake the re-organizing of house work, this occupation should take its rightful place as one of the best occupations for the average woman.

From a consideration of domestic service we naturally pass on to those occupations of girls which grow out of a knowledge of "domestic science." The study of domestic science is making itself felt in the homes of the country and is opening up many avenues of employment for girls. The management of clubs, hotels, restaurants, tea-rooms, cafeterias, and lunch-rooms in connection with colleges, departmental stores, and banks, affords employment for those who have the gifts and training necessary. Special cooking for invalids, the supplying of specialties, such as marmalade, pickles, preserved fruit, canned fruit and vegetables, salted nuts, cakes of various kinds and other dainties is work which is being carried on successfully by numbers of women and girls. The girl, in considering employment, should remember that she will be at an advantage in any specialized women's employment and that the world is offering her opportunities for good work which a few years ago had not been dreamed of. The occupation of house work, household management, cooking, all the arts of the home, will well repay the enthusiasm and energy of every girl who has a gift in this direction. What the girl with ability for this work needs to bring to her problem is, not only enthusiasm and energy, but originality and initiative. "I have a real gift," she should say to herself; "how can I make the best use of it?"

Universities have established departments of domestic science, and there are also domestic science training schools. Numbers of graduates find positions as instructors. Many other positions are open to the domestic science graduate. Practical experience is required in most of these openings. After graduating it is advisable to find a position as an assistant. In this way the young woman in this occupation will become fitted to hold the most responsible and remunerative posts. There are possibilities in household work and domestic science which have not yet been realized.

CHAPTER VIII

THE TEACHER

Two girls were playing a game of tennis together. One of the girls was a skilful player, but the other knew little of the game. In a few minutes the skilful player came to the side of the net where the other stood. "See," she said, "this is the way to hold your racket. This is the way to strike the ball." The unskilled player grasped the idea, and immediately much pleasure was added to the game for them both.

A singer was giving a lesson to one of her pupils. She explained to her carefully how to stand, how to breathe, and how to let her voice flow easily and naturally from her throat. The pupil's voice became to her thereafter something more than it had ever been before.

Two men in a business office were discussing whether or not they should undertake a new enterprise. One of the men, seeing that the other man had not yet perceived the principle underlying the business situation, drew a sheet of paper in front of them on the desk and made on it a series of calculations. "I understand now," the other man said, "I see the risk and how you have made provision for meeting it."

The skilful tennis-player, the trained singer, the able business man were sharing their knowledge with others, showing them how to make the best use of their powers. That is to say, they were teaching others. Every person is to some extent a born teacher, but some men and women make teaching their life work.

Many girls teach for a few years before entering some other occupation. Perhaps they earn money in this way to take a course at a college or university, and afterwards they may either return to teaching or enter some other profession. There are other girls who are what we call "born teachers." They love more than anything else, guiding, training, and helping children. It is no trouble to them, but rather a delight, to show and direct, gently, repeatedly, untiringly, along the path of knowledge. Girls who are born teachers should receive every encouragement to devote themselves to teaching until they have homes to look after and children of their own to teach. Many good teachers teach only for a few years and do excellent work. But it is to the "born teachers" that we must look for the happiness of the school and its highest development.

The girl who means to be a teacher should look forward to spending a number of years in school. She will enjoy this, for the teacher must be a student and must love studying. It may be that her family cannot afford to keep her at school. Then she can do what so many other girls have done. She can go to work to earn money for her own support, and while doing this she can save part of her earnings so that later she may return to school. The school vacation in summer offers opportunities for paid work, and every girl of energy and determination can find work to do.

The girl who is to be a teacher should never be satisfied with a minimum of learning. If this is her attitude toward school, then she should never be a teacher; because no girl or woman can be a good teacher who does not love to learn. The office of a teacher is a sacred trust, since she is responsible for the future well-being and happiness of little children. So if the girl does not love to learn, she should find some work other than teaching.

Provincial Governments in Canada have charge of education, and each Province has its own regulations, carefully framed, to provide good teachers for the children of the Province. The girl who is to be a teacher must pass a series of examinations, the first two of which are for teaching in lower grades and higher grades of the public schools. The graduate of a university has a standing which enables her to teach classes in high schools and collegiate institutes.

The girl may continue her studies while she is teaching in a public school, and she may either take her next examination without attending further classes, or, when she has saved enough money, she may return to school for a few sessions before trying her examination. The girl who has energy and ability and who loves study is often able to obtain an excellent education for the teaching profession in this way. It is necessary, however, to warn girls who find study very difficult, that it is doubtful if they should think of trying to pass this series of examinations. If they love teaching and have a true gift for it, they will probably be able to take the first examinations, which are comparatively easy. The higher examinations may be beyond their reach. This fact should not depress them. Their work is with the little children, and there is no better work in the world.

The most important qualities for a teacher are a sympathetic understanding of human nature, a keen sense of justice, and a sense of humour. These are great qualities, but the girl who means to teach should notice that they may be both acquired and developed. Any one who gives all her energies and gifts to teaching will find that the work is a strain. The teacher should not allow her work to become set in a fixed routine. She should guard against becoming autocratic and unprogressive. She should never cease to be herself a student. Each day should add a little to the sum of her knowledge.

She may begin the study of new subjects, and thus keep a certain freshness in her mental attitude. More important, however, than the knowledge gained from books, is her interest in the life of the community in which she is living.

The salary of the teacher varies according to the community in which she lives and the grade of teaching in which she is occupied. It may be taken as a general rule that teachers do not become wealthy. They are not highly paid, considering the time spent in preparing to teach and the quality of their work. Their salaries, however, almost invariably ensure them a fair average of comfort in food, clothing, and shelter, an opportunity to save, to continue their studies, to travel a little, and to enjoy their holidays, which are longer than the holidays of the average worker. A teacher's holidays are necessary for mental and nervous recuperation and should include some study and improvement in aims and methods of work. The rewards of the profession are not in money and leisure merely. Teachers have the respect and affection of the community to a degree enjoyed by few other workers.

If a girl begins to teach in the schools of a city, she will enter a thoroughly systematized and complex organization. In the city the teacher's salary is increased automatically year by year if her work is satisfactory. In towns and villages salaries are lower, but living expenses are lower also. In partly settled districts and districts where there is as yet little appreciation of the value of good teaching, salaries are low. Maximum salaries for women who have taught for a number of years in the public schools and have unusual ability as teachers may be as high as nine hundred or one thousand dollars. These women teachers, with their ability, would probably make more money in other occupations, but their work would hardly be of the same service to the community, nor would they have the same feeling of satisfaction in doing it. The salaries of women in high schools and collegiate institutes vary from seven or eight hundred dollars to eighteen hundred, two thousand, or twenty-four hundred. Women who are lecturers and professors in colleges and universities are paid amounts similar to the higher salaries in collegiate institutes.

The average salaries of women teachers in the public schools of Ontario for 1917 were as follows: Cities, $795; towns, $628; incorporated villages, $573; rural schools, $580.

Besides the ordinary teaching of the class-room, girls may be attracted to the teaching of special subjects. The girl who studies for kindergarten work needs to have an active imagination, a sympathetic understanding of child nature, a happy disposition, and both vocal and instrumental musical training. There are also domestic science teachers, teachers of special classes for handicapped children, teachers of manual training, sewing, millinery, music, physical training, arts and handicrafts, and commercial subjects. The girl of special opportunities and gifts may become a teacher of languages. Other girls may teach privately in households. Others, if they have capital and some business ability, may establish small private schools of their own in neighbourhoods where such schools are required. Recreation centres and playgrounds, settlements, the training of foreign children, call for unusual or special gifts and energies from girls and women who teach. There are also executive and administrative positions in large schools and school systems which may be obtained by women teachers of experience.

There are still discoveries and advances to be made before perfect training and education can be secured for our children. Girls who teach may hope to aid in making these discoveries. Patient work, constructive imagination, and enthusiasm are required in the great enterprise of advancing education. As an inspiration, the lives of great teachers invite young teachers of this century to follow their examples of devotion and leadership. It is not many years since a woman teacher in Montreal saved as many of her children as she could and stayed to shepherd the other little ones who perished with her in the burning school. The name of Sara Maxwell is an inspiration to every Canadian child who hears her story. She gave her life to protect and comfort her pupils and became one of that great number of teachers who have proved that theirs is a high calling.

CHAPTER IX

THE WORK OF A NURSE

There are many wise sayings about the trained nurse, two among which may be given here. One of these was spoken by a woman who is herself a distinguished trained nurse, and the other by a woman in a public position who has met many people and is a good judge of character. The nurse said, "Trained nursing will make a woman very good or it will harden her." The other woman said, "I have never known a nurse who was not glad to be a nurse and who was not thankful for a nurse's training." These two sayings show that the work of a trained nurse is no ordinary occupation. The girl who becomes a nurse-in-training is preparing to enter an employment which will have a great effect upon her character.

A girl must be twenty, in some hospitals twenty-five, years of age before she is accepted by a training school of good standing. If she prefers to enter a school connected with a children's hospital, she may be accepted when she is twenty. The work of a nurse calls for physical strength and endurance, and it has been found that girls under twenty or even under twenty-five are not strong enough to stand the strain of hospital work. A very strong healthy girl under twenty may say, "Oh, but I am strong enough to stand the strain." She is mistaken. It is not only physical strength which is required, but physical endurance, and these extra years are needed to develop this endurance. If a girl who hopes to be a nurse leaves school when she is seventeen or eighteen, the best work she can undertake in order to prepare for nursing is work in her own home. Another way in which she may spend part of her time profitably is in the reading of good books, so that she may store her mind with thoughts and information which will be helpful to her in dealing with her patients. No woman who is a nurse can be too well read, or too well informed in art, music, biography, history, and the public affairs of the day. If a girl, who feels that nursing is her real work, prefers to earn her living between the time when she leaves school and the day that she is accepted as a probationer, she may enter some other calling, and meanwhile may add to her useful knowledge both of people and of work. She should also save some money, for while the training of a nurse is not expensive, still as probationer and, later, as nurse-in-training, she will need money for necessary expenses.

The intending nurse should make a few financial calculations before she begins her course of training. The hospital will give her exact directions as to the clothes she will need for her work while she is a probationer. She will require some spending money, and she should be provided with a good stock of clothes, especially underwear, shoes, and stockings. When she is accepted as a nurse-in-training, she may be given by the hospital a monthly allowance which is supposed to provide her with clothes and the books required for her studies. This sum varies in different hospitals. Generally speaking, it is fifteen or twenty dollars a month. In any case, the sum will be hardly sufficient to cover all her expenses, although it is wonderful on how little money nurses-in-training have been able to manage. Some hospitals do not give their nurses-in-training any money and require that the nurse should pay a sum for her instruction. It is usual for these hospitals to provide nurses-in-training with uniforms, caps, and aprons.

Most training schools require from applicants an educational standard of four years in a high school or matriculation status. Young women who are college graduates may take the training of a nurse after they leave the university. The business girl or the girl in any other occupation who means to be a nurse and who has left school before reaching the necessary standard can prepare for her training by attending evening classes or studying by herself or with a friend.

The intending nurse should choose with great care the hospital in which she means to train. The standing of the hospital will have a marked influence onher career as a nurse. Some hospitals are justly famous for the excellent training which they give. The usual length of time required is three years. A number of hospitals, however, have courses of two years.

The time of probation lasts three, four, or six months. During this time the probationer will be tested for endurance, neatness, earnestness, and ability. No probationer who is untidy or who is wanting in personal cleanliness is accepted in a training school. The professional appearance of the nurse is essential to her success. Few women are more attractive in appearance than a nurse in uniform.

Nurses-in-training live in a nurses' home which is one of the hospital buildings. In these buildings the nurse will spend by far the greater part of her time for two or three years. The hospital is a world in itself, and the nurse will have few interests outside its walls. Most nurses regard their years of training as a time of growth and wonderful experience, and the average nurse is very happy during this time, although a great deal of the work is not pleasant and almost all of it is hard. The nurse learns that work of any kind may come within her province. She will have to do anything which helps toward the recovery of her patients or contributes to their comfort. Some of her experiences will teach her resolution and bravery. Speaking of such experiences a nurse once said: "As long as you can do anything to help, you can manage. It is the being able to help that matters." The life of the nurse-in-training is regular, and the hospital regime is such that as a rule nurses-in-training are healthy.

The nurse should have good health and a good constitution. In some cases, however, a girl may be in poor health because she has no definite occupation or object in life. Training as a nurse has often helped to establish good health. The girl who applies at a hospital training school requires a doctor's certificate, and the doctor will be able to tell her whether she is strong enough to undertake the work of a nurse. She should be a girl of strong character, steady nerves, clear mind, and good judgment. She must acquire the habit of obedience if she does not already possess it. A nurse, like a soldier, is under authority and has to carry out directions exactly as if they were commands. In her work she will need tact, discretion, and firmness, and with her firmness she must be always and unfailingly kind. Her voice and manner should be as pleasing as possible. No unkind or rough woman should ever have anything to do with the work of nursing.

Short courses in nursing are given in some cities by the Young Women's Christian Association. The St. John Ambulance also has given instruction in nursing for a number of years. Since the beginning of the War, various courses have been arranged for Red Cross nurses. The honourable work of what are known as V. A. D. (Voluntary Aid Detachment) nurses proves how valuable any good instruction in nursing is, not only for the individual, but also for the community. It is not too much to say that the whole service of nursing in the world would not have been adequate if it had not been for the training and work of volunteer nurses. The War has proved beyond all question the extraordinary value of the trained nurse.

After graduating from the training school, the nurse may undertake private nursing or she may follow her profession in institutional work. Private nursing is exacting, and the nurse must be strong and capable. Her hours are longer and much more irregular than when she was in training, and often she will be on her own responsibility. She will feel, however, that she is doing work of great value, and she will win the regard of many of her patients and their families. The good standing of the training school is an assistance to the nurse when she looks for cases. If she is favourably known to doctors, she is likely to have as much work as she can manage. Hospitals often engage their graduates to return for private cases. A usual charge for a graduate nurse is from twenty-one to thirty-five dollars a week according to the nature of the case. A nurse in private work cannot work uninterruptedly throughout the year. Her name is on a nurses' registry, which is generally conducted by an association of nurses or by a private individual. Returns from these registries show that the average nurse is employed about ten months in the year. Many graduate nurses earn from eight to nine hundred dollars a year in private nursing, while some earn a thousand or twelve hundred, but this is exceptional.

Nurses who are not graduates are sent out by some registries. Their charges vary according to the case. These women are sometimes called convalescent nurses and, in cases where a graduate nurse is not required, they fill a real need in the community.

As a general rule, a trained nurse does not continue in private nursing longer than ten or twelve years. Frequently, at the end of that time, her health necessitates a change of occupation. Others continue their work successfully for many years.

Many trained nurses prefer institutional rather than private nursing. Head nurses in hospitals receive from thirty to sixty dollars a month. There are also nurses who superintend private hospitals. A few nurses of executive ability, business knowledge, and experience in nursing, become superintendents of hospitals, but not of the largest hospitals. A number are heads of training schools. Such leading nurses receive salaries varying from one thousand to two thousand dollars a year, with living expenses in addition. The work of a woman superintendent who is a trained nurse includes the financial management, responsibility for the nurses, training of the nurses, the care of patients, and the oversight of the hospital. Few individuals are equal to such work and responsibility. Other trained nurses become matrons and housekeepers in private hospitals, sanitaria, and colleges. Some are district nurses. Public health nurses assist in supervising the health of a city and give instruction in cleanliness, sanitary science, and the care and feeding of infants. Private schools, colleges, factories, and departmental stores employ the services of trained nurses.

A few children's hospitals give short courses in training for children's nurses—an employment for which many girls are specially fitted. This course must not be confused with the regular instruction of the trained nurse, as it is not on a level with the profession of trained nursing. A children's nurse with hospital training will receive twenty or twenty-five dollars a month; in some instances such a nurse is paid higher wages.

CHAPTER X

DRESSMAKERS AND SEAMSTRESSES

The head of a dressmaking department in a large store in a city, when asked how she prepared herself for her position, told this story. "I never took any lessons; but I had always made my own dresses and my sisters'. I remember walking down the street of the little town where I lived, one day after my father died, and as I passed the door of the best dressmaking shop in the town, it occurred to me that the man in charge of the store had often said that he would gladly pay me good wages if I would work for him. I made up my mind while passing his shop that day that I would not work for him, but that I would open a dressmaking establishment of my own. I did so, and it succeeded from the first. After a few years I thought I should like to move to the city. I applied for the position here and was appointed."

A second instance shows how a girl may have ability which she has not at first understood how to use. In this case the girl was anxious to enter another occupation. She wished to be a painter and had studied for some years both in Canada and abroad. Needing to earn some money, she found that she could sell dress designs to a manufacturing establishment, but there was not a large demand for such work in the city where she lived. Accordingly, she and another girl, also an artist, took a studio in a city which was a centre of fashions, and together they worked on dress designs for exclusive shops. They both had some money saved, and one of the girls had a small, regular income. The first girl proved to have a very rare sense of colour and design. It is now her work to make colour combinations and provide the ideas for original designs, while the second girl, who is a good draughtsman, executes the coloured drawings. These girls are now recognized as two of the best costume designers in the city where they are working.

It is apparent, then, that the girl with good eyesight, clever hands, and a fine sense of colour and form, is likely to be a success as a dressmaker. But how is she best to prepare herself for her chosen occupation? She should practise sewing, either by hand or machine. She should cultivate steady application to such work, and she should not object to spending a good part of her time indoors. She should have a certain amount of taste and some ingenuity in carrying out her own ideas or the ideas of others. Manual skill, originality, and artistic ability are required by the successful dressmaker. The girl who means to make dresses for others, should, herself, dress quietly and in good taste.

If the girl is able to continue at school and has a natural gift for dressmaking, the best way for her to learn her trade is to spend some years at a technical school. Here she will be taught sewing in all its phases—fitting, finishing, designing, the choice and use of materials, and the business details of dressmaking. The dressmaker cannot learn her trade once for all and go on repeating operations which do not require originality. Styles change, and season by season she will have to adapt and carry out alterations in fashion which will tax all her ability. If she cannot give more than two years to learning her trade in school, she is still at a great advantage when she enters a dressmaking establishment. She will understand all the different processes and will be able to work in the various sections, thus gaining far more rapidly in experience than if she had had everything to learn from the beginning. Actual trade experience will teach her a great deal. If, however, she is obliged to leave school at fourteen, she should at least have had the advantage of the instruction in sewing which is given in the public schools. It is probable that she may be obliged, when she enters a dressmaking establishment, to act as a messenger girl. She should make sure, however, that she is not used for running messages only. It would be better for her to accept less pay, with the understanding that she is to be taught the details of dressmaking, than to earn more money and have no opportunity to learn. The more she tries to understand and imitate the work of experienced dressmakers, the better will be her training. The custom of having apprentices has fallen rather into disuse, and the girl will find the learning of her trade left largely to her own initiative. As soon as she begins to have some skill in the operations of the workroom, she should attend evening classes in sewing, fitting, finishing, and designing. She should wait, however, until she is sixteen or seventeen before she attends these classes. While she is learning from other dressmakers, she will have sufficient work for a few years.

The first work she will be given to do will be finishing the underside of dresses, felling and binding, sewing on buttons, pulling out basting threads, and working button-holes. After this, the younger workers begin to specialize in skirt-making, waist-draping and waist-finishing. The designing and cutting are the work of a head dressmaker. There are also sleeve makers and their helpers, embroiderers, and collar makers. One of the younger workers is called the shopper and is sent to wholesale and retail establishments to buy furnishings, trimmings, and materials of various kinds.

The working hours in large establishments are eight, eight and a half, and nine hours. Smaller businesses have hours from eight to six o'clock. Dressmaking is somewhat seasonal, and the dressmaker must reckon, to some extent, on slack time. Generally speaking, there are two dull months in summer and one in winter.

A messenger girl may begin at from five to eight dollars a week. A dressmaker who does machine work and who does not specialize in other work, may earn ten dollars a week. Other wages range, according to the worker's ability and the work she can do, from twelve to fifteen, and from sixteen to eighteen dollars. Head dressmakers who cut out and design, receive salaries of thirty dollars a week in large establishments, less in smaller establishments. In somewhat rare cases a head dressmaker is paid more than thirty dollars a week.

The experienced dressmaker, who is at the same time a good business woman, may conduct an establishment of her own which will bring her in anything from one thousand to six thousand a year and over. But she must be able to manage matters of capital and credit, understand buying, and succeed in winning the favour of her clients. Custom dressmaking is being increasingly limited to high-class and exclusive work. The small and highly specialized dressmaking factory is affecting the custom trade. Girls, therefore, who are thinking of dressmaking as an occupation, should examine opportunities in the exclusive factory, since this branch of the industry is becoming increasingly important.

Another department of dressmaking to which no reference has yet been made in this chapter is the work of the seamstress who sews by the day in the homes of her employers. If she is really a competent dressmaker, her employment is assured. But it is a mistake for a girl or young woman without training or experience, or without a dressmaker's gifts, to undertake dressmaking by the day. A dressmaker—to define the term—is one who understands cutting, fitting, and making dresses sufficiently well to undertake the occupation as a trade. A girl should be at least eighteen or twenty before she becomes a day seamstress. In this work she is on her own responsibility and is handling goods of some value, so that she needs judgment as well as knowledge. The rates of payment are from a dollar and seventy-five cents to two dollars and a half a day, meals included. Sometimes the home dressmaker may be paid even three dollars or more a day, but in this case she must be quick, and her work must be exceptionally well done. The ordinary seamstress should be a neat sewer and should know how to fit, but she is not expected to design or to make elaborate costumes.

CHAPTER XI

THE MILLINER

Millinery, like dressmaking, is partly a factory trade. But it is also, like dressmaking, carried on in shops and in departmental stores. The average girl is interested in hat-making, and is able to turn out a hat which she can wear with satisfaction. But a first-class milliner is really an artist. Her hands must be skilful and quick, her touch light and sure. She must have a sense of colour and form, and originality and creative ability. A girl who combines these gifts with business ability is likely to make a success of an establishment of her own.

Training for this occupation may be obtained in several ways. The girl who can afford to remain at school may take a course in millinery at a trade or technical school. She may then obtain a position in a millinery establishment as a maker of hats, and will receive a beginner's salary according to the quality of her work. She should have no difficulty in advancing rapidly in her occupation if she has the necessary gifts.

The girl who leaves school at fourteen may find a place as messenger girl in a millinery shop or a millinery department. Some milliners make a special point of training their own helpers, and any girl who enters an establishment of this kind will receive valuable instruction. There is a danger, however, that the girl in some shops will find her work confined to running messages. In this case she will not become a trained milliner and her prospects of advancement are poor. She should, therefore, see that she is being taught her trade. It is usual for an apprentice to work for two seasons without pay, and if she is being well taught she should be satisfied. In places where living expenses are high, as in large cities, girls are often allowed a small sum per week while they are learning.

The young milliner's first work is learning how to make bands for hats and to make and sew in linings. Making frames for hats follows—the frames are of wire and buckram. The girl has next to learn how to cover frames with materials of different kinds—silk, velvet, lace, chiffon, etc.—and she as a result learns to know intimately and to handle skilfully delicate and costly fabrics. From being an apprentice she becomes an assistant maker and then a maker of hats. She may then be promoted to the work of a trimmer. The work of the trimmer is considered one of the most difficult stages in the creation of a hat. The girl who aspires to this work must have an eye for beauty of line and she should know how to harmonize the trimming to the shape of the hat. In smaller establishments the trimmer is also the designer. The girl who has original ideas is always the most important in an establishment. For this reason the designer commands the highest salary.

Assistant milliners may earn wages varying from seven and eight to fifteen and eighteen dollars a week. In an exclusive business a first assistant may get as much as twenty-five dollars a week, but she will need to be a good saleswoman and a successful manager in the workroom. The milliner in charge of a department or one who is managing an exclusive millinery shop of recognized standing, receives a high salary. As a rule the woman who buys abroad and does so with judgment and skill is in receipt of the largest income that is given to a milliner. These cases are all exceptional. A moderate millinery establishment owned and managed by a woman is likely to produce an income of one thousand, fifteen hundred, or two thousand dollars a year.

Experience shows that ability to sell hats counts for almost as much as ability to create. Tact, skill, patience, must be combined with the genuine gift required to find the hat which will be most becoming to a customer, or to know how to alter a hat so that it may suit the taste of the purchaser. Once it is proved to a customer that the milliner has this gift, her custom is assured.

A point of the first importance to the girl who means to be a milliner is the fact that millinery is a seasonal trade. The spring and fall trade may give her employment for seven or eight months only in the year. In the better millinery establishments the girls are laid off without wages six weeks or two months. In large departmental stores other positions are found for the girls and they may be without employment for only a few weeks. But the girl must understand that if she is earning ten dollars a week for thirty weeks in the year as a young milliner her income is only three hundred dollars. For this reason it is wise for the young milliner to have a second occupation. She may spend her summer months working in an hotel as a waitress or caring for children or picking fruit. In the winter slack season she may find a position as a saleswoman. If she can afford to remain at home, she may spend the time in replenishing her own wardrobe, and sewing for members of her family. She may also get some orders for making hats from friends and relatives. She should use the slack season to attend classes in design and salesmanship, skill in which will increase her efficiency and her earning power.

CHAPTER XII

MAKING ONE'S OWN CLOTHES. HOME MILLINERY

In the chapter on "What Every Girl Needs to Know" we found how important it is that girls should have a good deal of general knowledge of the cutting and fitting of clothes, design, what constitutes right line and beauty, the characteristics and uses of materials, and what is called style, which is really often only good design and good workmanship. Girls should welcome every opportunity to learn skill and judgment in spending their allowances or their wages. The girl who buys wisely is able to make the same amount of money give her twice the return in value which a foolish girl who buys carelessly receives from her ill-considered investments.

It is a wise plan, therefore, for every girl to learn a good deal about dressmaking and to be able to cut out and sew many of her own garments. She should also study buying. The best teacher she can have in learning how to buy is generally her own mother. But sometimes her friends will be able to give her help in this way. Girls who work in factories where clothing is made, and girls in shops and stores, learn from their work when blouses, coats and skirts are skilfully cut and well made. But this is part of the general knowledge that every girl should have. One girl can easily help to teach another who in return will be able to assist her friend in other ways. Not to be equipped with this skill in dressmaking and in buying makes the girl largely dependent on others as far as her clothing and appearance are concerned, and in this way she may be placed at a disadvantage both in her work and in her life at home.

For the same reason every girl should learn something about the making of hats and of the materials used in millinery. To be able to make her own wearing apparel is one of the principles of economy for the girl. She may be able with this knowledge to provide herself with a becoming hat for a small amount of money. She will know, too, whether the amount asked for a hat is reasonable, and will often be able to resist an extravagance because she will be able to tell that she is being asked to pay a considerable sum of money for an article which is intrinsically not worth the expenditure. The girl who can make her own dresses, blouses and other wearing apparel and who is an adept in home millinery possesses knowledge which has a direct money value. She is much better off financially than any girl who cannot sew and who is not able to trim her own hats.

The wage-earning girl has often a very small income in the first years of her experience in paid employment. She can afford to spend only very small sums for her coats, blouses, skirts and hats. Often she tries to make her necessary clothing in the evening after her paid work is over. It is very difficult for her to do this if she has had no training in dressmaking or in millinery. But if she has learnt how to cut out and to sew and how to trim her own hats, work which otherwise would have been extremely difficult becomes interesting and successful. It is well to remember also that girls with very little money, if they must buy their clothes because they do not know how to make them, are compelled to buy only the cheapest things which wear but a short time.

For the worker who is well established in her employment and has a good income, home dressmaking and millinery become questions of health, time and energy. This worker should make the best use of her strength. It is often wiser for her to pay someone to do this work for her since she can afford to do so, though she sometimes may regret the days when she found time to enjoy making a blouse or trimming a hat. She has, however, the satisfaction of knowing that without this special knowledge of dressmaking and millinery she would not be able to buy wisely the wearing apparel which she requires.

CHAPTER XIII

TELEPHONE AND TELEGRAPH GIRLS

The telephone girl who enters her employment in a city gains the first knowledge of her trade in a school which is maintained by the company. She fills out an application, stating how old she is, how long she has been at school, and whether she is living at home or boarding. She should be sixteen or seventeen years old, and it is better if she has had one or two years in a high school. Her work will require accuracy, and she must be quick in thought and action. There should be no defect in her speech, and she should be at least five feet in height since she requires a good reach on the telephone board. Girls who go into this work should have strong nervous systems. The necessity for rapid and constant action, the strain on thought and nerve, and the call for resourcefulness and coolness, all of which are connected with the work of a telephone operator, are a constant drain on nervous energy.

The girl remains at the training school two weeks or longer and during this time she is paid by the company exactly as if she were at work. Payment varies in different parts of the country. But the girl at school generally receives a beginner's wages.

In small towns and country districts, the beginner learns to be a telephone operator by substituting for the regular operator. There is less pressure in telephone work outside of cities, and there is more room for initiative than in a large city exchange.

Telephone exchanges in cities are large airy rooms, well lighted, well kept and ventilated. These rooms are pleasant places in which to work, and the telephone company provides lunch and rest rooms for its staff. A matron takes general charge of the girls, and a dietitian looks after the food provided and advises the girl employees with regard to their health. In the rest room are comfortable chairs and a lounge. The management provides tea, sugar and milk and the dishes in the lunch room. The girls may buy cold meat, bread and butter, biscuits and other food for a small charge. The hours are eight in the daytime and seven for night operators; this length of working day is regarded as the utmost which can be required from girls in telephone work. There are two rest periods in the day, besides time for lunch.

In the school the young operator is trained to answer requests for numbers, to make and break connections, and to keep account of calls. She is taught to enunciate clearly and to speak courteously and agreeably. She learns to know the board and its numbering. The board is divided into sections and each section comprises a complete multiple. Each multiple consists of eight panels, the panels being divided into "banks." Each bank contains a hundred "jacks," every one of which represents a customer. When a connection is made, the telephone operator connects one jack with another by means of a cord and two plugs. By the time the girl is an experienced operator, she has become accustomed to the little flashing lights constantly appearing in front of her, which mean that a connection is asked for.

The operator in a city begins with ten or eleven dollars a week. In two or three years if she is a satisfactory operator she should be earning fifteen. A supervisor receives from sixteen to eighteen or twenty. The duties of the supervisor are to walk up and down behind the girls at the board so that she may be certain they are giving satisfactory service, to check delays, and to help in difficulties. For instance, if a call comes through from a fire or accident, the operator will often give it in charge of the supervisor immediately so that there may be no delay. The chief operator who is responsible for the whole service and who has the management of the working force is paid from twenty-four to thirty dollars a week, according to the size of the exchange and the amount of work involved.

Skilled operators are often employed in private exchanges and when they are competent they earn from twelve to fifteen dollars a week or more. The most important switchboards are in hotels, apartment houses, public and governmental offices, stores and private offices. The work is often exacting and in many cases requires executive ability and resourcefulness. The operator is expected to answer calls, make connections, answer questions and keep account of the number of calls made. Sometimes important business depends on the good-will, executive energy, judgment and quick thought of the girl at the switchboard. A young woman of strong vitality and good mind—where she has responsibility and can use initiative—finds this work fascinating. Such a worker sometimes wins important promotion because she is able to show that she can manage both people and critical situations and has business and financial judgment.

Telegraphy also offers employment for girls, but not to the same extent as the telephone exchange. The automatic machine has made a considerable change in this occupation. The Morse operator is now employed to a much smaller extent than formerly. There are still a number of men and women who are Morse operators, but they are being replaced to a certain extent by girls who operate automatic machines. The machines are extremely ingenious and do away with the necessity for the operator to understand or use a code.

Telegraph companies in some cases maintain a school for the instruction of Morse operators, and girls who enter telegraphy receive a weekly wage while at the school, as is the case with girls in the telephone school. In some cases instruction is given during work in the operating room. Schools are at central points only. If the girl who wants to learn telegraphy lives in a small town or in the country, she must be taught by the telegraph operator. A number of girl operators are to be found in country offices. The writer remembers specially two of these girls. One was in a telegraph and cable office down by the sea. She had been a telephone operator and had learned telegraphy from the telegrapher in the same office. The other girl was in an inland railway office, and had learned from her brother, who had held the position before her. Both these girls were earning good salaries.

The hours in a telegraph office in the city are from eight to six, with a luncheon hour. The room in which the girl is at work is crowded with machines and people. There is a good deal of noise and a great pressure of business, much of which is important. The girl needs to be thoroughly interested in her work and to have steady nerves in order to do well in telegraph operating. It will take her several years to become a competent Morse operator. An automatic machine is operated by a typist. The companies apply a simple psychological test by means of which they can judge whether the applicant has the power of concentration necessary for accuracy and success in this employment.

Many girl operators have charge of agencies in different parts of towns and cities. These girls have agreeable work under no great pressure in a quiet place, although with a certain amount of responsibility.

The wages paid girls who operate automatic machines vary according to the age, ability and efficiency of the workers, and the locality where the work is done. Typists may begin at seventy-five dollars a month, with increases up to eighty-five. Girls in training as Morse operators are called check girls and may receive thirty, thirty-five or forty-five dollars a month with an increase in the second year to fifty dollars. Women who are Morse operators belong to the same union as the men and receive the same wages. In larger places they begin at eighty-five dollars a month and receive increases up to one hundred and twenty-three dollars and twenty-five cents.

Both telephone and telegraph operators are in a sense public servants, and may win the respect and gratitude of their clients. They sometimes suffer from a lack of appreciation of their really arduous work; but as a rule the public recognizes good service. These workers often show loyalty under trying and exacting circumstances. On many occasions girls have risked death from fire and flood by staying at their posts to warn others of danger. During the Great War there have been instances of telephone and telegraph operators performing services as faithful and as brave as many of the deeds on the battlefield.

CHAPTER XIV

HAIRDRESSER AND MANICURIST. WAITRESS

Hairdressing and shampooing, manicuring and chiropody, are almost exclusively the work of girls and women. There has been a decided improvement in these employments, and any girl who takes a serious interest in making herself a thoroughly trained worker in one of these lines of work, provided she has the gifts which are needed, is likely to find her occupation becoming more and more necessary and esteemed.

To be entirely successful in work of this kind a girl should have engaging personal qualities. Just as a doctor or nurse with abundant personal vitality gives health and encouragement to patients by being in the same room with them, so the girl who gives massage after a shampoo quiets and soothes the client with whom she is working and who has come in for a rest as well as to have her hair shampooed. A girl with this power to soothe is a helpful person. She will never lose a customer who can remain with her if the customer has once experienced the difference between an ordinary treatment and the superior work of the girl who is gifted by nature with a personality which both soothes and invigorates.

While a girl may begin her training as young as sixteen, it is better if she is nineteen or older. Some experienced women say that no girl should begin work of this description younger than twenty. She should apply for a position as a helper in a shampooing and manicuring establishment or with a chiropodist. Sometimes the pupil is expected to pay a fee of twenty-five dollars or more for three months' instruction. But in many good establishments it is held that the work of a beginner is very soon worth something. It is not necessary, therefore, for the girl to pay a fee in order to become trained. She may find a place where she will be paid a fair wage for a beginner within a short time after she has been accepted. But if the beginner pays no fee for her instruction, the head of the establishment will expect rightly that the assistant will remain in her employ two or three years at least so that she may repay the time and care which have been given to her training. In a year and a half a good assistant should be earning from ten to twelve dollars a week, and in two or three years her weekly wages are likely to be fourteen or sixteen dollars. If she takes some responsibility in managing the work and workrooms, she may earn as much as seventeen or eighteen dollars a week. In some establishments tips are allowed. The girl should understand, however, that as a rule wages are lower where tips are permitted. It is better for her to be employed in the best kind of establishment where the highest wages are paid. In such an establishment tips are unusual.

The helper is likely to begin by taking care of the rooms and toilet articles, washing brushes, combs, etc., and carrying out miscellaneous orders. The attractiveness of the rooms depends on the perfection of these details.

After some years spent in a good establishment the young woman may undertake appointment work. She should choose carefully the district in which she means to work, so as not to interfere with any other shampooing or manicuring business. She should not take away customers who belong to the business where she was trained. She will need to have some money saved in order to provide herself with the necessary articles which she has to carry with her, as well as tonics and lotions. Her expenses will also include a telephone, carfare, printed cards, and so on. She should estimate her expenditures carefully to determine how much she is making over all expenses by the week, the month, and finally by the year. The summer months are likely to be slack, and this should be taken into account. She should arrange her appointments so that she may make the best use of her time and energy, and she must keep appointments punctually. A successful business of this kind may realize a weekly return of from twelve to eighteen dollars. Such a worker by the time she has saved some capital to invest may be able to start an establishment of her own, but she should do so only after a careful calculation of the expenditure required.

The modern tea-room has changed to some extent the occupation of the waitress. The modern lunch room in the same way makes a feature of the class of girls who attend on customers. They are expected to be especially quiet, deft and well mannered, and they should be dressed with that entire suitability to their occupation which is a mark of the well-bred girl. These girls have often been brought up with no special occupation in view—possibly they had not expected to earn a living by paid employment. But the opportunity comes to find work in a tea or lunch room, which is owned or managed by a woman friend, and they gladly enter on their new occupation, pleased as every normal girl should be to be busy and to earn an income. It is possible for the girl who has duties at home to spend part of her day as a waitress in a lunch and tea room. The same gifts and knowledge which make her a success in her work at home cause her to be prized as a waitress. She understands how a table should be set. Quickly and deftly she lays the table after each customer has been served. Her touch and movements are noiseless and pleasing to watch. She is interested in what each customer wants. She is thoughtful and has a good memory, is good tempered and not impatient. She has an instinct for placing and arranging food so that the man or woman at the table feels that he or she is being waited on by an intelligent, well-mannered person. In spite of the high standard of the service required, the pay is rather small. It may not even cover all the girl's expenses. She has the advantage, however, of limited hours and leisure to carry on her duties at home.

The work of the regular waitress is in an hotel, restaurant, women's club, or in the dining rooms connected with apartment houses and private hotels. Women who work in such places should be neat and smart in appearance and should wear dresses of a uniform standard, generally black with white aprons, cuffs and collars. A good home training is of great assistance to them in their work. They should have common sense and good judgment, and be polite to customers and fellow workers. Perseverance, intelligence and physical strength are required by waitresses. A girl who is naturally erect, with a good carriage and graceful walk, is at an advantage in this occupation. She needs to be kindly and thoughtful and to take pleasure in serving her customers. She has to understand and remember her customers' checks, and the amount of the checks she hands in ought to equal the average cash sales of other waitresses. Many customers make a point of coming to the same waitress every day, and she should remember where they prefer to sit and how they like to be served.

One advantage in this work is that the worker is given two, sometimes three meals, in addition to her payment in actual money. In a number of establishments the tipping system prevails, which provides a girl with an added source of income. The average Canadian girl, however, dislikes being tipped, and there are many objections to the tipping system.

CHAPTER XV

FARM WORK FOR WOMEN

Among those who choose work on the land as a special employment are girls and women in the country who have the opportunity to give either part of their time or all of it to farm work, and others from the city who prefer an outdoor life. The problems of the city girl or woman who wishes to engage in farm work are how to acquire skill and experience in her business, capital for land and equipment, labour, transportation and a market. The girl on the farm can solve these problems with an advantage of fifty, seventy-five, or one hundred per cent. as compared with the girl who migrates from town or city to carry on independent productive work in the country.

Most girls and women in the country are familiar with farm life, and know beforehand what they require for success in any kind of farm work. Eggs, poultry, cream, butter, vegetables and fruit are sent to market by women who are also home makers. There is, also, a growing movement among a few able country women to make their productive work so extensive as to constitute one-half or one-third of the whole work of the farm. Thus in some instances a third of the farm land may be devoted to a poultry farm; and its management is in reality an extensive business, undertaken with all the thought, planning and attention which are given to a large farm project. Productive work of this character is successfully carried on by a few women.

A restricted number of women who have lived previously on farms and are thoroughly familiar with farming conditions have undertaken farm management successfully. Such women are exceptional and there is no present indication that this employment will be taken up to any large extent by women. The farm manager must be strong enough to do her own work when she is unable to procure assistance, and she may at times have to live alone.

The girl who lives on a farm and who has the endowment needed has an exceptional opportunity to engage in productive work on her own initiative. She should secure a plot of land on the farm for her own use. When the other labour on the farm is being done, it takes little extra time and exertion to do what cultivating is necessary on the girl's plot of land. In this way she can arrange with little trouble and at little expense for any manual labour which is beyond her own strength. A girl or a woman who goes into the country from the city to engage in independent productive work finds the problem of labour one of her greatest difficulties. In this as in other respects the girl whose father or brother is a farmer is at an advantage.

A young woman thus situated has her land secured as her share of family good will, or at a small rental after her business has begun to pay. An arrangement, as has been pointed out, can easily be made for the manual labour required. She has an opportunity to learn her work thoroughly, and to experiment, before she actually goes into business. She can arrange for necessary fertilizers at an advantageous rate. Finally, the means of transportation to market, and the market itself which has been found for the products of her father's farm, often can be used for the products which the girl has chosen to raise on her plot.

If she is particularly attracted to flower-growing, the girl on the farm may devote herself to growing violets for market. She must study violets carefully. She should be an authority on the subject. She should learn to understand their appearance, habits and diseases. She should know just what to do for her plants, how to feed and tend them, how to get the best results, how to make a violet blossom the best blossom of its kind that can be offered for sale. Besides this, she must know how to pick violets, how to grade them, how to pack them, and when and where and how to send them to market. It would appear practically certain that if the farm produce is sent to market, the girl may send her violets, properly handled and packed, at the same time, and she will be likely to find a ready demand for her flowers, if she offers fine violets for sale.

A woman who is a bee-keeper writes as follows of how a woman may acquire skill in this country employment. "A good beginning for the woman who is to keep bees is to read Maeterlinck's 'Life of the Bee.' If after reading such a book the girl or woman who thinks she would like to be a bee farmer is still further interested in bees, then she may decide to go into bee culture.

She should offer herself as apprentice to an up-to-date bee-keeper as soon as the spring work begins and stay with him to the end of the season. The following spring, if still inclined for the work, she should buy from her employer two, four or six prosperous colonies of bees. If she prefers to do so, she may take a short course in bee-keeping at the Ontario Agricultural College, Guelph.

Characteristics which the bee-keeper needs are a cool head and steady nerves. She should also have determination to succeed and some indifference to pain.

Some difficulties which may be encountered are bad choice of location, winter losses and poor seasons. There is heavy lifting to be done, but generally a lad in the neighbourhood can be hired to come for part of the day to help. By ingenuity a good deal of the lifting can be avoided.

The advantages of bee-keeping are a healthful, outdoor occupation which takes one's mind off real or imaginary worries, with a certainty of small profit in spite of set-backs and large profits in favourable seasons. Bee-keeping is a good occupation for the woman who is suited to it, but not every woman can be a successful bee-farmer.

When the bee-keeper's work calls for larger space she may rent outyards from farmers in the locality. Her market is likely to be found near where she lives. Those who know that she keeps bees will bring her orders. Bakers use a considerable amount of honey. If the bee-keeper lives near a good road for motorists, she may put up a sign saying 'Honey for sale,' and the demand probably will be larger than she can supply."

A woman who moved from the city to the country is now favourably known as a grower of flowering plants for marketing. She began as a student of wild flowers and became a wild flower specialist. The first money she made from flowers was earned as the result of her wish to give to a missionary society. She bought seeds from a reliable dealer, parcelled them out in selected varieties, and sold the packages. She also planted the seeds in her own garden and studied the plants carefully. The occupation grew until it took up most of her time. A larger garden was obtained and expert knowledge was acquired gradually in the growing of perennials. The demand for her plants grew steadily. When she made a change from a city garden to a country place, greater expenditure was necessary, and the cost of labour became a serious item. But the beauty of outdoor life and love for her special work have counter-balanced all difficulties. Her business is now well-established and successful.

The principal difficulty, according to one authority, for girls and women in the business of farm production, is that they have to find out that they must learn to understand facts with which they think they are already familiar. A girl on a farm, for instance, makes up her mind to undertake poultry farming as a business. She may be of the opinion that she knows all about poultry, from the kind of buildings which ought to be used to the nature of any disease likely to attack poultry. This believing that she knows all about poultry, or vegetables, or fruit, when in reality a good part of the knowledge she has is imperfect, will be a great obstacle to the girl in such work. The girl of good judgment will set to work to study her subject with enthusiasm and perseverance. As a rule people who understand a subject best are slow to believe that they know all there is to know on that subject.

The girl or woman who hopes to leave town or city life to engage in work in the country should have a certain amount of capital, not less, it has been said, than five thousand dollars; but the amount of capital required depends on the locality. A greater amount than five thousand dollars may easily be necessary. She will also need a small income, since she may not be able to support herself wholly by this work for a number of years, if indeed she does so ultimately. She should be strong physically and should enjoy manual labour. She should be fond of an outdoor life and of whatever kind of work is involved in her enterprise. She should like animals and growing things, and be able to live without constant social stimulus.

The Ontario Agricultural College at Guelph has trained a number of young women in different branches of agricultural production. Short courses may be taken during the year, and the special classes during the summer months are most useful and popular.

The special need for production which developed during the War induced many girls and young women, including a number of women students from universities, to volunteer for farm work. During the summer months some hundreds of young women engaged in fruit picking and worked in canning factories under government supervision, and were lodged in club houses managed by the

Young Women's Christian Association. Others undertook various forms of work connected with agriculture, meeting with success in their employment and with public approval. In the summer of 1918 a special course of instruction for young women in farm work was arranged at the Ontario Agricultural College, and later regular courses were established throughout the year. Women now may qualify for the degree of Bachelor of Science in Agriculture at the Ontario Agricultural College and at Macdonald College, Quebec. Wider opportunities for women in agricultural employment are thus being recognized.

CHAPTER XVI

THE LIBRARIAN

Library work, although unusually attractive, does not employ a great many workers. The work is pleasing, it is valuable to the community, and the associates with whom the librarian works are trained and intelligent.

Almost any girl who loves books and reading may be attracted to library work. She should test herself first to see if she has other necessary qualities before she makes up her mind to train as a librarian. A girl who really dislikes detail and who fails in detail work is hardly likely to succeed in this occupation. The usefulness of a library depends on a constant routine of work faithfully performed by its staff. An assistant does not spend her time in reading new books, although the best type of library worker must always find time for reading. The librarian is working for the interests of others. Her mind should be sensitive and alert to the needs of the public. She must love books, but it is equally true that she should be a lover of humanity. If she feels only impatience and irritation when she is asked to leave some routine work to find a special volume for a boy or girl, man or woman worker, or some old person who has come into the library to read, then she should not be in library work.

The standard of education required for a librarian is constantly being raised. The entrance examination to a university is often required as the minimum in academic training. A librarian cannot be too well or too widely educated, and it is generally agreed that sound scholarship is required in a library. This point should receive careful attention from the girl who is thinking of library work. A position as an untrained assistant is not easily found. More and more, it is becoming a profession for men and women who are college graduates and who in addition have taken professional and technical training in a school for librarians.

Training in library work may be obtained in different ways. The girl may enter a library as an assistant where she will be taught the methods of the library in which she is working. As has been said, she should be interested in books and people. She should be neat, accurate and quick in her work, widely read and well informed. The payment which she will receive may not at first be sufficient for her support, so that she will need either to have saved some money earned in another employment, or to be able to live at home, remaining partly dependent on her own people until she has acquired skill as a librarian.

After she has worked in the library as an assistant, she should attend classes in a school for librarians. The library training school, conducted under the authority of the Department of Education for Ontario, has a course of several months, with lectures, instruction, and practice work. Library boards frequently grant leave of absence to librarians and assistants so that they may attend this school. Application for admission should be sent to the Inspector of Public Libraries, Department of Education, Parliament Buildings, Toronto.

Library schools in the United States give courses of one and two years in all the branches of librarianship. These schools require for entrance either that the applicant has a standing equal to the second year in a university, with a knowledge of French and German, or a university degree. Any young woman who is a college graduate and has a certificate from one of these library schools is likely to find good employment in a library.

The technical training which a library assistant must acquire, either in a library or at a library school, includes the classification of books according to subject, the cataloguing of books, some knowledge of binding and repairing, the arrangement of books on shelves, the use of open shelves, how to serve the public, filing and use of periodicals, how to use reference books of all kinds, preparation of reading courses for clubs, how to make the library useful to boys and girls at school, and practice in the children's library.

In a small library, while the work is not greatly divided, one librarian, possibly with an assistant, must carry on all the work of the library.

In large libraries, the work is divided into a number of departments, each of which is in charge of a responsible head, who may have several assistants. Over all the work of the library is the head librarian.

The administrative side of library work calls for executive and business ability. The best experience for a young worker whose gifts are in this direction is to be obtained in a small library. She may, if she has training, become director of such a library and she will gradually win promotion to a larger library, unless she finds that the work where she is suits her capacity better.

The cataloguer labels the books as they come in and prepares cards which will represent the books in the catalogue. A book may be asked for under several different classifications, and the skill of the cataloguer is required to decide how many cards are needed and under what headings the books should be listed.

The reference librarian has work of an altogether different character. She is constantly in touch with the public. All kinds of questions are brought to her. The reference department sometimes maintains a telephone service; that is, clients may telephone inquiries to the library and the information needed will be looked up and telephoned to them within a reasonable time. The reference librarian requires a complete knowledge of books of reference, encyclopaedias, bibliographies, and dictionaries of all kinds, and she must be skilful in their use.

The circulation librarian has charge of the collection of books to be loaned to the public. She must be familiar with the collection and should understand the tastes of those who use the library. Book exhibitions and announcements are under her care, and she generally has charge of a number of assistants.

One of the most pleasant and yet one of the most exacting positions in a library is that of librarian in the children's room. The children's librarian must be fond of children and should be able to control and influence them for good. She should have the wish to instruct and she needs a rich endowment of imagination, since this is necessary in order to understand children and to sympathize with them.

Other openings for librarians are in scientific schools, medical schools, and in some law firms and business houses where the keeping and filing of documents are of special importance. Librarians in such positions are on their own responsibility and sometimes do important reference and bibliographical work. Civic and engineering libraries, municipal libraries, libraries on music, architecture and art, the cataloguing of prints and pictures, special work in bibliography and indexing, offer in a few cities opportunities to trained and gifted librarians.

Salaries of from six to eight hundred are not uncommon for library assistants who have training or experience. In a number of positions the library may be open during limited hours, or on certain days only. But when all a librarian's time is required an effort is made to pay a salary which will ensure for the librarian a reasonable standard of comfort. The better paid positions have salaries of eight or nine hundred up to twelve, thirteen or fourteen hundred for women librarians in charge of branch libraries, heads of important departments, and chief librarians.

A woman's work in a library offers opportunities for service and self-improvement. The profession is fairly well paid. It requires careful training and constant study. Enthusiasm, ability and initiative may make the librarian one of the most useful and influential citizens in the community.

CHAPTER XVII

WORK FOR THE GIRL AT HOME

We have been referring so far to girls who are earning a living in paid employment, working usefully and happily in almost all the occupations which make up the gigantic output of national activity. Many thousands of girls at home are doing household work which is just as necessary to national well-being.

Chapter Eighteen on The Home Employments, which follows this chapter on Work for the Girl at Home, is intended to state more fully the importance of the occupation of home making. The present chapter is planned to suggest lines of remunerative work for girls who are helping in home making, but who require spending money and a healthy, active interest in life and people outside the home.

Every girl who is helping to make a home may be certain that she is one of the world's necessary workers. The home people are dependent on her more directly and to a far greater extent than the work of the office or factory is dependent on the girl who is a paid employee. The girl at home may not seem to have anything definite to show for all her daily tasks. As one home maker said of her own work: "Just a lot of dishes washed and a lot of meals cooked and eaten." But the working efficiency of all the members of the household is dependent on this work, and not only their working efficiency, but their happiness as well. The output of a factory can be expressed in so many thousands of dollars and cents. But the work of a home is expressed in a spiritual and mental, as well as in a physical, total.

The girl who is doing necessary work for the home should be paid an allowance, unless the family income is so limited that it is impossible to arrange for one. It should be understood in every case that the work of the girl has a money value, as well as a value which cannot be recompensed except by affection. When the family income does not permit of an adequate allowance, happily the girl is often able not only to support herself with work which allows her to continue her home occupation, but to make a contribution to the upkeep of the home. The girl at home who is making an income from other work should save part of what she makes for investment, for some special training, or for recreation and travelling.

The home girl should remember that her expenses are small. She does not pay for board and lodging as is generally the case with the girl in paid employment. There are a hundred small incidental expenses met by the girl who goes out to work which are not necessary for the girl at home. She has no set hours to keep and she has time to sew, to make clothes and trim hats without over-tiring herself as the wage-earning girl often does if she is her own dressmaker and milliner. The working clothes of the girl at home may be very simple. She does not need to go out every morning to her work, and for this reason can dress more economically than her wage-earning sister, and still be neat and fresh.

Let us suppose that the girl at home needs to earn an income, either small or fairly large. The first step she should take is to think carefully over her own possibilities, and the possibilities of the neighbourhood in which she lives. What can she do that is worth payment, and where can she find someone who is willing to buy what she has to sell?

She may have a gift for sewing and dressmaking. If she is really capable and can do satisfactory work, she may easily build up a small business among her friends and their friends in the making of smart blouses. The girl should always remember that poor work is never worth while. Her blouses should be better than anything her clients can buy at a store. They should have distinction and style of their own, and a fineness and individuality which the stores cannot rival. If her gift is undeniable but her workmanship is poor, she should take lessons at a school of dressmaking and make herself a first-class worker. She may possibly undertake dresses, although blouses generally are more useful and more possible for the girl at home. In the same way, the girl with a gift may specialize on hats, but her hats must be professional in workmanship and individual in style.

Perhaps the girl at home is a born cook. Home-made bread is always in demand. But it must be the best that can be produced. A specialty in home-made cakes of certain kinds may be made profitable. Candy-making is often carried on successfully as a home industry. But the home girl who does work of any kind for profit must have business sense. She must itemize her expenses accurately. Cakes or bread which have not turned out well should never be offered for sale. To do so is not fair to the worker, for one of her most valuable assets should be the fact that her work is always satisfactory.

The work of the home has changed greatly in the last fifty years. Once rugs, carpets, blankets, yarn, soap and candles were made at home. If the girl can find a market for home-made rugs she might make rug weaving a profitable employment. The same is true of soap. In these days of thrift and economy, days when work must be better done than ever, a girl might induce the women of a neighbourhood to let her become a local soapmaker. But she would have to be certain of herself and of the work. A co-operative canning kitchen would be a great benefit to the women of any community, and two or three home girls who could count on a certain amount of time for this work could manage the kitchen. This work would be specially suitable for girls in a small town or country district. They could arrange for a market in a neighbouring town or city. The arrangement could be made through a local Women's Institute or Home Makers' Club. "Canning circles" have been managed successfully in some parts of the country. If the girl wants a small business of her own in preserving fruits and canning vegetables, she may develop a market in her own neighbourhood. If her home is in the country she may arrange to supply a store or a number of housekeepers in a neighbouring town, or she may help to form a circle and work with other girls.

Selling flowers, choice fruit and poultry may be made money-making occupations by either country or city girls. First, the girl should know her specialty. She should not merely know something about it, but she should make herself an absolute mistress of it. Her flowers should be fine in quality and colour. They should be properly handled and properly packed. To begin with, of course, they should be properly grown. Nothing is left to accident in a successful business, and the home girl should see that she is not in any way behind professional dealers in her line. If she is selling hand-picked fruit, the people who buy from her should know that they will receive only the best. Those who buy are willing to pay a higher price for any specialty which is the best of its kind.

Girls whose interests are of a different character may find other paying employments. To find the employment depends largely on the study of one's capacity and one's neighbourhood. Is there any opening for a lending library? Then the girl who is fond of books and reading and who understands the average taste in reading, provided she can find a little capital, may start a lending library. It is possible that there may be a library in the neighbourhood which would be glad to engage her services a few hours in the day. There are villages and country districts where a girl living at home could make a success of a small library.

The girl with a turn for keeping accounts might become a visiting bookkeeper. Doctors and dentists often have their accounts kept by someone who is not altogether in their employ. A good business connection of this kind might be worked up in a neighbourhood. Or a girl might answer the dentist's or doctor's doorbell and telephone during certain hours in the day. She could give attendance in his office at the same time. A girl is often able to find employment for some hours a day in a store in the neighbourhood of her home. A village store which is also the post office may engage her as an assistant for part of the day.

Mothers in a suburban neighbourhood are often glad to have some girl at home look after their children one or two afternoons in the week. To undertake work of this character successfully the girl should be fond of children and able to manage them. If she can tell stories well, she might form a circle of children to attend a children's hour. A visiting mother's help would be a boon in many neighbourhoods.

The possibilities of paying employment for girls at home who have initiative and some spare time are almost limitless. The girl's ingenuity is the only measure of what she may do in the way of paying work. The field of success of two such girls of the writer's acquaintance is the lovely, old-fashioned home garden. One girl has made a specialty of poultry. Her stock is of the best. She sells eggs, both for household use and as "settings." The other girl grows roses in the garden and from her own success as a rose grower she has become a seller of rose bushes. They are both happy in their employments, and they continue to be home makers as well as business women. The income is not the only benefit which the girl at home receives from such work as this. Her work brings her into contact with other people, broadens her interests, increases her usefulness, and, moreover, is often a recreation. The home-maker needs outside interests. The girl at home is never dull, or unhappy because she is dull, when she has an avocation in addition to her work and life in the home.

To unite her home-making and her other employment successfully, the girl should learn how to organize her time. A girl, for instance, might look after poultry while she waits for the kettle to boil. The same time might be taken for work in the garden. Heat that is used to cook dinner will help to can or preserve. The day's work should be planned carefully if time is to be put to the best use.

CHAPTER XVIII

THE HOME EMPLOYMENTS

The more thoroughly women and girls understand paid work outside of the home, the more clearly they recognize that work in the home is of high standing, intellectually, artistically and spiritually. The most able women in outside work are constantly looking back to the home, hoping that they may be able to introduce into home life and management much that they have learned in other pursuits.

One of these women whose name is associated with a famous business success, in writing of her own work recently said: "I believe that work which is most commonly thought drudgery can be made attractive and beautiful if it is approached in the right spirit, and I feel more than that—that until all women are awake to this, and really enjoy their work—whether it is running a home and bringing up their children, or being out in the world in business—they will never be as efficient as men are in their field."

We should be careful then to know how a girl should equip herself for the home employments. If she will look back to chapter five, "What Every Girl Needs to Know," she will find that in order to develop into a young woman able to meet the problems, work, responsibilities and joys of life, she should know how to keep herself and other people well. To keep herself well, she should understand the values of food and how to prepare food; she should know how to dress, which includes knowing how to make and mend clothes; and she should know how to rest. In order to keep other people well, she must know what food should be given to babies, to people at work, both men and women, and to old people. She should also be able to judge whether they are properly clothed and cared for. If possible, every girl should have some knowledge of nursing. She may not be a trained nurse, but she should have some of the knowledge and skill of the trained nurse.

One of the finest of the home employments is this great work of caring for people and keeping them well. One of the functions of a home is to preserve the health of its inmates.

Fortunately, any girl who wants to learn the art and science of home making may learn at home or in school, or she may go to special classes where all these domestic subjects are taught. There is hardly any study which is more delightful, because one has the pleasure of working with one's hands as well as studying. A girl who is a good cook, and knows how to cut out clothes and sew them, has a good part of the knowledge of the home-maker.

What else does the girl need to know before she can feel that she is properly trained to have charge of a home? The girl should be prepared to find that home-making requires a varied and very interesting training. The best home-maker needs a thorough knowledge of household accounting. The business girl understands that the factory, the store and the office can not be managed successfully unless the manager understands all about the bookkeeping of his business, for the books of the business should show the exact condition of the enterprise. The home is not a business and yet it requires some knowledge of business.

Much of her own happiness and usefulness and the happiness and usefulness of others will depend on her knowledge and ability to handle an income. She should read the best books and magazines on household management. If the girl has no books of her own she should ask for advice and help at the public library.

The home maker has many interests and an endless variety of duties. She needs to study—and if need be to take some action to try to control—the sources of food supply for her household. She must decide what manufacturing work should be done in the house. Are bread and cake to be baked at home? What preserving and canning are to be undertaken? How much clothing is to be made in the house, either with or without help? In every case the decision has to be made according to individual requirements. It may pay one home maker to bake her own bread; in the case of another, her time and strength may be needed in other ways. The problems of mending, and of taking proper care of household furnishings, are part of the duty of the home maker. She should also be an expert buyer, and should be able to judge of the quality and price of fabrics and of their suitability. If she employs a houseworker, she must be able to plan the work of her helper. It is important that the home maker should be fair to everyone whom she employs. Wages, hours, food and shelter, treatment and standing, should all be of the best character that she can give. The very nature of a home is based on right human relations. Nothing that is unjust or unkind should be tolerated in the management of the home or its relationships. The home is not managed for profit, but for human well-being. This fact alone places the work of the home maker among the first and best employments.

By far the most important function of the home is the care and training of children. No girl or woman can have too great a talent, or too careful a training, or too fine a personality, to devote all she has to the care of little children. It is a very wrong thing for anyone to undertake ignorantly, or to fail to be interested in, the best care of the health and feeding of infants and their early training. All girls who have had anything to do with the care of babies know how very delightful babies are, and how worth while it is to take care of them and to win their affection.

The twentieth century girl has to deal with two aspects of home-making, one of which is an old aspect revived, while the other is a principle new in its application to the work of the home. We have been taught by the stern necessity of the Great War the importance of the food supply of the world and the household. Every woman who is a home maker should have, if possible, a small garden in which to grow vegetables. Even if she lives in an apartment, she may arrange to have a garden allotment in co-operation with others. Gardening is one of the oldest of the home maker's employments.

The principle which is new in its application to the work of the home is co-operation. So far home makers have carried on their affairs independently, each woman very largely by herself. Suppose a group of ten women, practical, experienced home makers, with sufficient business sense to recognize fair business dealing, were to decide to arrange for some of their home making work in partnership. A great deal of the household buying of coal, bread, flour, canned goods (when buying canned goods is advisable), sugar, and other groceries, meat, poultry, butter, eggs, etc., might be carried on to great advantage in partnership. Canning, preserving and baking might be undertaken by one or two of the members of the group, or a professional worker might be engaged to do this work for the ten members. The actual expenses should be shared fairly and a considerable saving would be effected when the output was distributed amongst the members. In the same way, the co-operative group might arrange for household help. One skilled houseworker might assist with the work of three or four households. Washing, ironing, cleaning, dusting, mending, dressmaking, sewing, shopping, and the care of the telephone, could be carried on either partly or wholly by members of the group in return for other service, or by paid helpers who in every case should be reliable experts.

The principle on which successful co-operative work is based is the forming of a small group of well-known and trusted individuals to carry on work either in production, or buying and selling, or in both, with the sharing of expenses and the elimination of commission and secondary profits. Co-operation is admirably adapted to the work of home-making. The girls of the twentieth century, with courage, cleverness and enterprise, may bring a new blessing to the work of the home through the use of co-operation.

While the home-maker recognizes that her first interest is the work and the life of the home, she must also be interested in the affairs of the day. The home is the heart and kernel of the affairs of the world. It is a mistake to try to get rid of the work of the home; the right way is to enjoy it; just as a doctor, an actor, a writer, a manufacturer or a merchant enjoys his or her work. The affairs both of the home and the world belong to the woman home-maker. We should take pattern by English and French women, for the English woman is keenly interested in political affairs and is able to discuss them with understanding, and the French woman is admired by all because she is her husband's business partner and can continue the business in his absence. A partner with responsibility is better and happier than a worker without responsibility, and of infinitely more value to the community than an idler without an intelligent interest in life.

No true home can exist without the recognition and love of spiritual interests. Home life is intended to promote the growth of kindness and mercy. The woman of the home must also help in providing recreation for her family and herself. Thus home becomes the best and happiest placein the world and is worth all we can give in time, energy and love to make it so.

CHAPTER XIX

**JOURNALISM. WRITING. ADVERTISING. ART. HANDI-CRAFTS. DESIGNING.
PHOTOGRAPHY. ARCHITECTURE. LANDSCAPE GARDEN-ING.
HOUSE DECORATING AND FURNISHING. MUSIC. ACTING. DANCING.**

Many girls who have definite gifts are specially interested in the occupations described in this chapter. As a rule, the girl with a decided talent has no difficulty in choosing the employment which she wishes to follow. But she sometimes is in doubt as to whether her ability is sufficiently great to justify her in choosing an art rather than a handicraft, or an art rather than a profession, or whether her gift should not be used in a directly practical business pursuit. One of the purposes of "The Canadian Girl at Work" is to teach the work of whatever kind may be interesting, and that the standing of the worker depends on the skill and perfection with which the work is done. Good art is found in many forms, but never except as the result of work, devotion and a gift. If the girl, in any artistic employment, helps to make the ordinary surroundings of everyday life more beautiful and more suitable she is using her gifts to advantage.

The girl who wants to write may find a suitable and enjoyable field in journalism. Some instruction in journalism is given in colleges, more often in connection with college papers than in any other way. But the usual method by which a girl is taught journalism is by working on the staff of a newspaper. Such positions are not easily found. Application may be made at newspaper offices for a regular position when one becomes vacant. While she is waiting to obtain regular work, the girl may write special articles and submit them for publication. We may take for granted that she enjoys writing, but she should be able to choose subjects on which to write. One of the first questions that an applicant for newspaper work is likely to ask is: "What shall I write about?" This question the writer must learn to answer for herself. She should know what is interesting and worth writing about. The journalist, besides enjoying writing and having some gift of expression, should be keenly interested in people, and should have enthusiasm for her work. The hours are long and the rate of payment not particularly high, but the true journalist is always in love with her work. Positions for women on newspapers are varied in character. Some women are general reporters and take assignments from the city editor. Others are in charge of a woman's page and may have one assistant or more than one, working under their direction. Some are special writers, covering a certain amount of general work and having a specialty in addition, such as music and drama, book reviewing, a page for children, fashions, market reports for women, and so on. An assistant on a woman's page may begin at ten dollars a week, and as her work increases in value she may receive twelve, fifteen or eighteen dollars a week. The woman journalist in charge of a woman's page is paid as a rule from twenty to thirty-five or forty dollars a week. Few women journalists are paid larger sums.

A number of other positions are held by women in connection with weekly newspapers, magazines and publishing offices. Salaries vary all the way from ten or twelve to thirty or forty dollars a week. The average salary for the woman journalist who has proved her ability is in the neighbourhood of twenty-five dollars a week. Many newspapers and some printing offices employ girls as copy holders. These girls begin at a weekly wage of seven, eight or nine dollars, and when they become expert, receive higher wages. The best paid positions for women proof readers are held by those who have proved their ability to compete with men expert in the trade. Women proof readers belong to the men's union and their wages are the same as those received by men.

An employment which is becoming more important for women journalists and writers is the writing of advertisements. Much advertising is addressed almost exclusively to women and women have proved that they can do work of this description to great advantage. Salaries are high as compared with salaries in other women's employments. The work is difficult and requires a distinct gift, besides a knowledge of how to write and of what is being written about. The woman who is doing advertising writing needs accurate knowledge of a number of special fields, such as fashions, the history of costume, period furniture, and so on.

Work for the girl who is gifted with an unusually fine sense of colour and form is developing rapidly. To be a painter, a woman should have an outstanding gift, and it is generally necessary for her to have an independent, or at least a supplementary, income. Many young women painters add to their income by teaching, and girls who live at home are able to continue the study of painting for their own pleasure and in part for an additional income. The training of a painter is long and costly, and while the gifted girl has happiness in her work, the occupation of an artist is exacting, although it may not seem so to the public. Girls with artistic gifts may find employment in illustrating, designing, bookbinding, handwrought jewelry, woodcarving, embroidery, and in weaving from original designs. The girl who is attracted to photography may obtain instruction in a photographer's studio, but the artistic photographer will have to depend largely on herself in developing the possibilities of her work. A number of women have achieved success in artistic photography.

To work successfully in any of these occupations, the artist must be trained and should have special gifts. Training is obtained partly in schools, partly in studios at home and abroad, and from working with other artists. Some of these artistic occupations pay well; in others payment is variable and more or less uncertain.

The woman architect needs a special gift and should be trained as thoroughly as possible in draughtsmanship. Her next step should be to obtain a place as draughtswoman or general assistant in an architect's office. Promotion afterwards will depend largely on individual ability.

Architecture and houseplanning are fields of work not yet occupied to any large extent by women. Girls with gifts for work of this character should be encouraged to enter these occupations, provided they have perseverance. It is always difficult to enter a new field, but a few women are already successful architects, and the advantages which should be possessed by women in designing houses are obvious. When a woman plans a house she considers it from the standpoint of a home and takes into consideration the nature of the people who are to live in the house and also the kind of work they will do both in the home and in the outside world.

Landscape gardening has, as yet, been developed little in Canada. There are, however, a few establishments carrying on such work and in one or more a woman is a partner.

House decorating and house furnishing have also been entered on as professional occupations by women. House furnishing in particular offers a promising field for girls with the necessary training and endowment. Many girls have ability for this work, and as the employment is being developed commercially, the opportunities for girls in house furnishing should increase with some rapidity.

Payment in all these fields of artistic work depends not only on the ability and skill of the worker, but in particular on the degree in which the products of her art are planned to meet the needs and desires of a large public. The individual worker who expects her work to find its own public is far less likely to have a steady income than the worker who is employed by some large firm. If the artist or the worker in handicrafts feels that she must work alone, or if she works better by herself, then she should have either an independent income or an alternative occupation; otherwise she will need a well-developed business sense in order to handle the products of her skill to the best advantage financially.

In music, the gifted girl may be a teacher, or may appear in public as a player or singer, or she may combine teaching with public appearances. Teaching music has been systematized to a marked extent. Many young musicians who teach are engaged on the staff of the conservatory or academy where they obtained their instruction. Musicians who appear in public generally possess, along with musical ability, a more or less impressive personality. A number of teachers who have made a decided success are in receipt of good incomes. A performer or singer needs to have unusual ability to earn a large income. Women musicians not infrequently make fine accompanists and may devote themselves to this branch of their art. In general, what has been said of the remuneration in other arts applies to music. But the systematizing of the teaching of music by institutions has a tendency to steady the income of the music teacher. Training of the best kind is long and costly, but any other kind is unsatisfactory.

In order to attain standing as a professional actress a young girl should have special physical training, voice culture and a broad literary education. She should know something of singing and dancing, and she should learn how to walk well and how to speak correctly and impressively. Part of this training may be obtained at schools of dramatic expression which are often connected with conservatories of music. The people of the stage work harder than the average trained or untrained worker. Their hours are longer and they endure more discomforts. There are few spectacular successes, and still fewer genuine reputations for genius in dramatic interpretation. Seasonal unemployment is prevalent in this occupation. Salaries seem to be large, but very few are large in reality. If we reckon the number of weeks throughout the year during which payment is received, it appears that few actresses earn a good income. A young woman of decided gifts may become an individual entertainer.

Dancing has recently come more into favour as an occupation, regarded both as giving physical training for health and as an art. The teaching of art dancing is undertaken by some conservatories of music and also by individual teachers.

All work of an artistic character requires an endowment of imagination, sympathy, insight, and artistic ability. The artistic worker gives a great deal, and does not enjoy or suffer temperately. It is impossible to do good work unless the whole being is thrown into the effort. Unless the artist possesses financial, as well as artistic, ability, the pecuniary reward is likely to be uncertain. But the individual with decided gifts rightly is dissatisfied in any other occupation.

CHAPTER XX

BANKING. LAW. MEDICINE. DENTISTRY. PHARMACY. CHEMICAL INDUSTRY. CIVIL SERVICE. SOCIAL WORK

Among girls at work and at school are those whose mental capacity is developed strongly. They enjoy thinking out problems. They analyze situations, because they want to understand why some particular fact happens to be true. These girls may be executive and practical, but they are always thinkers. If possible, they should remain at school in order to continue their studies. But although a girl who is intellectual may have to go into paid employment early, there is no reason why she should not eventually find her way into work for which she is better fitted.

Employment for the intellectual girl is varied, just as the intellectual girl herself, according to her individual capacity, is fitted for a number of different occupations. Banks have long employed girls as stenographers and a number of young women have held junior clerkships. But now the work of a ledger-keeper or teller is sometimes given to a woman, and there is a prospect for the intelligent girl with capacity for financial affairs to find a position in a bank, suited to her gifts. There are a few women in accountants' offices. The number of women who act as insurance agents is increasing, and it is considered that they have special advantages in insuring other women. A small movement, therefore, has already begun to introduce women into the higher branches of business and finance. In order to be successful in financial work, a girl will need to prepare herself as carefully as possible. She should understand something of business law and should be familiar with the machinery of banking and credit. The study of economics and popular government are part of her preparation. Women who have taken a university degree in economics are already influencing the fields of work which may be entered by the girl with a good intellectual endowment.

Women lawyers are doing good work in many of the larger cities, especially in the United States. The training required is long and somewhat expensive. There is no reason why a woman lawyer who has training and the legal instinct should not be a useful and successful worker. After graduating, she may find herself confined to office work altogether. If she has greater capacities, she may have difficulty in making opportunities for using them. Occasionally she may find employment in government service in connection with laws regarding children and factory work. Work in social service has attracted the attention of some young women to the study of law. In dealing with family difficulties through a "settlement," the social worker becomes impressed with the importance of understanding what legal redress may be obtained for some just grievance, and applies herself to legal study. Work among immigrants and foreigners unable to speak English is also encouraging the study of law by young women who are social helpers. This field of employment for women is not likely to be large, but it is growing.

The woman physician is an important social force in modern life. Some medical colleges require for admission a university degree, so that the course of training may cover seven or eight years. As a rule only girls who are strongly attracted to medical work and who are specially gifted for it, undertake the study of medicine. In addition to university work and medical school training, the young woman doctor if possible should spend some time on the staff of a hospital and should take postgraduate study either before beginning private practice or shortly after. For the first few years she may hardly be able to meet her living expenses. She may, however, obtain a position as a school physician or with an insurance company. The woman physician needs strength, health, a fine nervous system, idealism, self-control, unselfishness, and knowledge of human nature. Every fine quality which she possesses will be of service in her work. Her ideals cannot be too high, but they must be balanced with common sense. She needs also to be gifted with intellectual force. Her patients should have confidence in her skill and also in her character.

Dentistry offers to women a good although restricted field of employment, and so also does pharmacy. The woman dentist needs scientific accuracy, mechanical skill and good nerves. Her training is shorter than that required by a physician and will cost less. Her first employment may be in schools. Work with children offers the woman dentist special inducements; she may find employment doing children's work for another dentist. When she opens an office of her own, she will need a thousand, fifteen hundred or two thousand dollars in order to make a successful beginning. The woman pharmacist requires to attend a college for two years and to have had experience in a drug store before she can obtain a certificate. Accuracy, skill and carefulness should make her a successful druggist. If she has business ability, she should be able in time to manage a business of her own.

Young women who have graduated in science from universities are finding openings for chemical work in a number of industries. One girl who has specialized in botany recently discovered "a growth" which was injuring the quality of paper turned out by the mills of a paper company; she was able to tell the manufacturer how he could solve his difficulty. The chemical expert is constantly increasing in industrial importance. Teaching and laboratory work, therefore, are not the only employments open to the girl with an aptitude for scientific work.

A number of able women find employment in the Civil Service. They are required to pass a Civil Service examination. College graduates hold positions in the higher grades, while many women clerks are employed as stenographers and in minor positions. The statistical office, forestry, trade and commerce and the labour department, all need expert assistants. While few of the higher offices are held by women, still women with special knowledge and ability are being employed in increasing numbers by the government.

The income earned by professional women is likely to be comparatively small at first. These occupations are all full time employments and require the undivided attention of the worker. After some years of steady application, the professional woman is fairly certain to receive a reasonable, even a good, income. Two, three, and four thousand dollars may be regarded as incomes which may be obtained with reasonable certainty by women who are successful in their professions.

The intellectual girl should choose her work wisely. She is a good student and while she is in training it may seem to her that she will have no special difficulties of any kind to face.

When she comes to follow her occupation in everyday life, she will find that personal initiative, judgment, and executive energy in affairs are as valuable as the ability to master a problem in her study or in the laboratory. If her studies have left her isolated from human nature, she will find this want of understanding and sympathy a heavy handicap in whatever occupation she may enter. Scholarship cannot be made fruitful in everyday life unless it is used in the service of humanity.

One of the modern employments for young women of education which is increasing rapidly in its scope is to be found in social work. A broad general training and a special interest in humanitarian work are required by those who enter this occupation. The missionary and the deaconess may be regarded as forerunners in some sense to the modern social worker. Many Canadian women of the finest aspiration have become missionaries in distant lands; women physicians have accomplished work of great value as medical missionaries. The deaconess of to-day may be a graduate of such training schools for social workers as the Departments of Social Service and Social Science in the University of Toronto and McGill University. The special training of the social worker includes lectures in economics and sociology and the history of philanthropy, discussion of social problems in classes, and "field work" under the guidance of experienced workers. Positions for those who take training in social service are found in "settlements," and in connection with "Big Sister" associations, and Charity Organization Societies. Welfare departments in stores and factories indicate the growing importance in modern industry of work which has to do with social factors in employment. The trained social worker may find a position as secretary, statistician, visitor, investigator, lecturer, dietitian, nurse, or as a clerk or executive officer, in child welfare, civic improvement, or family relief work. Young women who mean to undertake such work should have, not only training, but common sense and idealism. Salaries are sometimes low, and much valuable work is contributed to social betterment enterprises by young women who live at home and are able to give their time and work free or for small remuneration. There are, however, a number of well-paid positions in connection with social service work.

CHAPTER XXI

GOING INTO BUSINESS FOR ONE'S SELF

Responsibility is something in which we all should share. If girls will observe people, they will see that human beings grow and become better able to work and help others through the exercise of responsibility. The girl or woman at work who feels her responsibility and is able to act on her own initiative is more valuable than the worker who always has to be told what to do. By gradually learning how to take responsibility, the girl becomes fitted to go into business for herself.

In the first place, few girls actually enter paid employment or business life with the intention of becoming independent proprietors. It is only after some years' experience of work that the idea occurs to them. A trained nurse may have been in private practice three or four years before she begins to think that she would like to own and manage a private hospital. For the properly qualified and equipped woman, this is a good business enterprise. A number of nurses are conducting excellent private hospitals. The work is exacting, the hours are long and the responsibility is heavy. But any girl who thinks of going into business for herself should know at once that all these conditions are true of every independent business that is worth while.

The business woman requires a precise technical and financial knowledge of the business which she means to enter, and she needs as well originality, a fund of ideas, courage, initiative, imagination, that feeling of capacity for responsibility and enterprise which is like love of adventure, judgment, nerve and character. She should not be too excitable and yet she ought to be keen. She should not be easily disturbed and she ought to be a steady worker. Above all, she requires to be able to deal with people, both customers and employees.

Instances of women who have been successful in business enterprises may be quoted which do not seem to conform to the requirements specified. But if they are examined, these instances will show that the women in question have fulfilled the conditions of success almost exactly as described. A woman has succeeded, for instance, in managing her own country inn. She was in a totally different employment before she started this successful enterprise. But she had already bought, built on, and sold with a margin of profit, three or four other properties. She had learned how to buy land to advantage in the neighbourhood of a city. She bought her present property, choosing a few acres which were already in fruit or in use for growing vegetables. There was an attractive, large, old-fashioned farm house on the premises, the property was near a railway station and situated on a road constantly used by motorists. Other enterprises of the same kind were studied by her. The food provided was made a specialty. Every expense which could be lessened in connection with the property was considered. A flock of poultry was kept. The fruit was either sold or put down for winter use in the inn.

In almost every instance the successful woman of business enters on her new enterprise in a small way. A girl begins by making and delivering lunches to the staff of a large office building. Later she adds other buildings to her list. She sells cakes, sandwiches and preserves from her own home. Having saved some capital, she embarks on a down-town tea room. Every detail of her business is planned as it expands and the management is entirely in her own hands. The successful management of a large business would have been impossible for an inexperienced girl, but it comes easily to the young business woman.

In the same way a nurse began a business preparing supplies for doctors. Soon she added invalid cookery to her other work. Her venture developed into a business partly catering, partly a dining club, and in part a depot for surgical dressings and home made cooking for invalids. Another woman has inherited a large catering business from her father. It was a considerable business when she became manager, but she had gone to work with her father as soon as she left school. Still another woman has established a system of hairdressing businesses. She began with one room in one city. Her business has been extended to over forty cities. No chance good fortune can account for successes such as these described. Managing ability, foresight and character are responsible for a great part of the achievement. The woman in each case made the discovery that the best commodity of its kind offered to the public in the right way must bring success, if the business enterprise itself is well managed.

Examples of the wise judgment of women in business are found in every large community. A girl who makes good marmalade for home consumption began to make and sell this product in a small way. She is now part owner of a large business. A woman who went into a factory as an office helper proved to have a gift for designing dresses. After spending a number of years in the employ of the firm with which she began work, she has gone into partnership with a woman dressmaker in a small specialized factory. A large wholesale fish business is owned and managed by a woman, whose knowledge of the business, including sources of supply and distribution, is entirely adequate.

Women who own and manage business enterprises when they succeed often do so because of their womanly qualities. There is no conflict between capable thorough work and womanliness. The normal woman has always a capable and helpful side to her character. She generally retains in affairs her gentleness, considerateness, and patience in dealing with all sorts of people. No quality is more important in business than a natural ability to understand and sympathize. A woman's ideas may be original and her knowledge of business details exact, but it is her power to work with others and to make the best of them which is the highest part of her business ability. Many of the businesses owned and managed successfully by women are connected with food, clothing, health, physical, mental and moral training, and personal well-being. The woman's advantage in business has to do most frequently with perfection in detail, personal supervision, knowledge of the highest home standards, and with making her commodity a little the best on the market. The best women in business excel in making conditions for their employees ideal. They plan to give their workers opportunities for education and training, and sometimes help them to start in business for themselves.

CHAPTER XXII

NEW WORK FOR WOMEN

One of the best known doctors in the country has chosen a special trained nurse to act as his anesthetist, that is, she accompanies him and assists in giving his patient the anesthetic when he is about to perform an operation. This girl when she entered the training school of a hospital had no idea that she would specialize in this way as an assistant to a famous surgeon. Her work is but one of the many examples of the usefulness of the trained woman worker. Varied opportunities in employment may be discovered by girls who are in earnest in finding the best work they can do.

A number of the new employments for women are connected with food, clothing and home making. The woman who fits herself to be a food expert may make a good income as a writer or lecturer, provided she has the necessary gifts as well as knowledge and skill. A food expert is sometimes employed in large departmental stores. Such a specialist is often found in charge of the dining-room of college residences. Dietitians are a necessary part of the staff of a hospital. The woman who qualifies as an expert on food is entering an occupation which is being recognized as of the first importance.

A visiting household expert who is competent to advise in the arrangement of household work and who is skilled in household accounting is a new worker in the oldest occupation for women. A food demonstrator is sometimes sent out by the government to teach canning, preserving and drying, and to explain new household processes. Women experts in poultry keeping and vegetable growing are also in government service. Women specialists have made a study of public marketing. Many women have made a success of the business of catering, of tea and lunch rooms, and of food specialties such as mushroom growing, raising squabs, preserving, pickling, and spicing fruits. In hotels, there are women managers, chaperones, hostesses and matrons. The old-fashioned boarding house is still a useful institution, and the girl who will undertake to keep house for a group of professional women on a co-operative plan is a modern worker likely to find remunerative employment. Any woman who has the capital to establish a well-arranged, well-organized home where expensive, high-class board may be obtained, in a city, or in the neighbourhood of a university, is certain to attract as many clients as she can accommodate.

Clothing and house furnishing offer fields of new work for women. The expert shopper in these departments is already in demand. An adviser in dress for women has made her appearance as a paid worker. Many women could save time, trouble and money if they could go to an expert for consultation about their clothes. A girl who is a specially good shopper should be able to build up a business among her friends.

Some women have made a success of high class laundry work. Girls who will undertake fine washing and mending of delicate fabrics are in demand. There is a greater need for the expert who will take classes in health exercises for women. Teachers trained in the Swedish gymnasium system are likely to find employment. Others are required for children who need special care. Courses of training are already planned for teachers of this description, and the occupation is likely to develop considerably. Social work is constantly requiring helpers in new departments. Investigators, secretaries, statisticians, lecturers, health workers of various kinds, are employed by social organizations. Welfare workers have made their appearance in factories. Employment departments of factories and shops are offering work to the woman who is an expert in employment. Others are in the service of civic and government employment bureaus. The vocational adviser is to be found in colleges and is employed by organizations of a benevolent character.

Rent collecting as an occupation for women was begun in Great Britain by Miss Octavia Hill. A woman in this country with capital invested in an office building, who has had business experience, manages her own building and collects the rents. Other women are employed as managers and agents for apartment houses. The real estate business has been entered by women who sell real estate, and accompany prospective tenants to houses and apartments. Other somewhat unusual employments for women are publicity writing in various commercial and public campaigns, and lecturing on various phases of modern life. Women are also commercial travellers, conductors of entertainments, pageant managers, window decorators, brokers and financial advisers, theatrical managers and producers of plays. They find employment as civil engineers and in research work of various kinds. Women have succeeded as conductors of foreign tours, and as lecturers on current events for women's clubs.

Some of these occupations may appear out of the way, and even romantic, to the girl who is choosing her work, or who is already at work in some paid employment. But in every case, the pioneer worker needs special training and experience. New work requires more originality, perseverance, and if possible better preparation than may be necessary in standard employments.

In conclusion, a word may be said to the girl or woman who has been at work for some years. She should take stock at intervals of the work she is doing, and of her prospects and possibilities. Let her devote some clear thinking as to whether her work could not be re-arranged to the advantage of her employer and herself. Purely routine work is scarcely ever as well done as it might be. She should ask herself, "Can I improve my work? Is there any new line in which I can develop? What special knowledge and skill have I? Am I using all the capacity I have? Does my work need to be changed or reorganized?" The girl or woman at work should not be satisfied with a superficial answer to these questions. It is generally possible to improve one's own work, by thinking about it carefully and by trying.

CHAPTER XXIII

MONEY AND WAGES

The weekly wage on which some girls live comfortably will give others only the bare necessaries of life, and sometimes not even that.

The girl's real wages are what she is able to get for the sum of money she is paid in exchange for her work. Before she can judge whether her wage is good or poor, she must know how much her board and lodging will cost, the cost of clothes, and the total amount of her other expenses. She should know what additional advantages there are in the place where she is working. If there are disadvantages, she should consider them also before she can tell whether the wage offered is a good or a poor wage. Local prices, and the difference in the cost of living between one place and another, must be learned by the girl at work before she can estimate the value of her wages.

During the time when she is becoming skilled in her occupation it is difficult for the girl at work to support herself entirely. If she is living at home, her family will help her. But she should always remember the girl who is not living at home, and should feel that it is her duty not to lower this girl's wages below a living standard. Every girl at work should make an effort to know what a living wage is in the place—town, city or country—where she is employed. Wages for skilled workers should be of a good standard, that is, the wage paid should be sufficient to make the worker efficient and comfortable. Even the beginner should have a living wage.

Prices of food, clothing and board, and the other expenses which one has to meet, are different in town, city and country. When the girl wage-earner changes from the place in which she lives, she should find out beforehand as accurately as possible how much she will need to live on in the place to which she may be thinking of going.

If we do not think accurately and carefully about what we earn and what we spend, we shall likely always remain undeveloped in judgment and character, and shall not be able to take the responsibility which should come to every mature person.

A girl worker in one employment may necessarily have a different scale of expenses from a girl at work in another occupation. For instance, it costs the average stenographer more to keep up her standard of efficiency than it does the average girl in a factory. The stenographer also has to spend more time and money in preparing for her occupation. A girl in a factory who is earning twelve dollars a week is better off financially, therefore, than the stenographer earning twelve a week. A woman physician may have a yearly income of two or three thousand dollars. A teacher who has an income of fifteen hundred dollars a year may be better off financially. The physician has to pay the rent and upkeep of her office; she must have someone to answer her telephone and to take messages; she may need a conveyance so that she can get about to her patients. Her training and the equipment she uses in her work are more varied and expensive as a rule than those which are required by a teacher.

We should remember that while what we earn is important, there are other considerations as important. The joy of the worker in her work is the first consideration. The born teacher, like the born doctor, is happier in her own employment. An income is a necessary possession, but it does not give that happiness which work alone can give. Very few of us work for money altogether, while many of us work to earn a living, which is a different thing. To be self-supporting through work which we enjoy is one of the greatest blessings of our existence.

It is impossible to state an amount which will represent accurately a living wage for girls who are beginning work in all the towns, cities or country districts of Canada. At present a living wage in a city may be nine, ten, eleven or twelve dollars a week; in places outside cities it may vary as greatly. Girls at work should look for an employer who recognizes reasonable standards and pays such wages as far as possible. The more loyal girls are to such employers the better working conditions will be for everyone.

Skilled and highly trained workers require, and receive, wages far above the sums mentioned in the preceding paragraph.

The girl should estimate the value of her yearly income. This is important. She may be a milliner and have steady employment for only thirty or thirty-five weeks in the year. If she is paid a weekly wage of twelve dollars, her yearly income will amount to three hundred and sixty or four hundred and twenty dollars. She must find some other occupation for the rest of her time or her total income will amount to three hundred and sixty dollars, or four hundred and twenty dollars and no more.

The trained nurse who is paid twenty-five or thirty dollars a week when she is on a case, will make a mistake if she forgets that she will not be able to work without intermission throughout the year. She may be engaged in her employment only forty weeks in the year. Nurses may earn no more than eight or nine hundred dollars in twelve months. Even the most capable factory worker does not earn her highest wage every week in the year. She should be careful to reckon her income by the year, not by the week.

The girl at work exchanges her yearly income for food, shelter, clothing and a number of other requirements, such as doctor's and dentist's fees, carfare, and washing, holidays, recreation, savings, etc. If she earns twelve dollars every week in the year her income will be six hundred and twenty-four dollars. Out of this she may pay five dollars each week for board, or two hundred and sixty dollars a year. If she spends between one hundred and twenty-five dollars and one hundred and fifty dollars for her clothes in the year, she will have about two hundred dollars for other needs.

What she uses her money for gives to the girl the real meaning of her wages. Her income means food, clothing, and a house to live in. Besides that her income means many small expenses, a little holiday and recreation, a little kindness to someone, church collection, a gift to someone who is in need, some small pleasure for the girl herself. It should also mean a savings account. Something will be said about saving in the next chapter. But here it may be said that if we spend everything we have from day to day, we are left with little choice in spending. Choice in spending is a test of the girl's character. We may choose to spend our spare money for candy. But if we do we shall probably not be able to buy a volume of poetry which we should love to keep and treasure. We may need a warm coat, but the money we might have had for it we spent for a second expensive blouse when we had one pretty blouse already. It was money we had saved which helped us to go to a course of lessons in gymnastics, and that course may have cured a tendency to headache.

The average girl hopes that her wages will increase, and this is right. An employer once said of the amount that he was willing to pay his most useful employees: "I feel that if a girl is not able to make a good bargain with me for her work, she will not be able to make a good bargain for me with others." The best and surest way for the girl to increase her wages is to think out some plan for increasing the value of her work, and then if necessary to say to her employer that she has been able to make her work more valuable.

A word of warning about wages may not come amiss here. If our wages are too low, the best way to go about raising them is to act ourselves, not to expect others to act for us. The best results are likely to be obtained by giving your employer some increased advantage, and by seeing at the same time that he gives you an equal advantage in your income. But never feel ill-used, because that lessens your happiness and your power to help yourself. Remember it is your own difficulty and you are the person to find the way out.

CHAPTER XXIV

SPENDING. SAVING. INVESTING

There is only one way by means of which we may know accurately how we are spending our wages. To know this we must keep accounts. Perhaps the girl has an impression that accounting is dull and troublesome. But this impression, if she has it, is a mistaken one.

This chapter on Spending, Saving and Investing is not written to keep the girl from having what she wants. It is written to help her to make the most of her wages, so that she will get the most use and pleasure from her spending. A pretty blouse does not make up for the prettier colour that ought to be in the girl's cheeks; it rather makes one notice more readily that the girl herself is not looking her best. To be well dressed and well cared for, to make the best of herself, a girl should learn to keep accounts and to plan her expenditures carefully. She has often seen a man poring over his business books, because he knows that by doing so with good judgment he can improve his methods. Similarly, the time a girl gives to the study of her accounts will also be to her advantage.

One business woman who has made a study of her expenditure has the following list of headings for her private account book: Board and lodging; clothes; laundry; dentist and doctor; car tickets and stamps; contribution to family life; books, magazines and papers; church and benevolence; gifts and entertainment of friends; holidays and travel; recreation, candy, music, and the theatre; study; clubs and societies; miscellaneous; taxes; saving and investment. The girl at work can usefully make a study of these headings since they, or others of the same character, are used by women in business who desire to lead normal, generous and helpful lives. The business woman just mentioned says that the money she has for her income would give her no satisfaction if she had not people of her own to love and if she were not helping to take care of them. From this statement any girl will understand the meaning of the heading "contribution to family life" in this business woman's accounts.

The girl at work, however, can begin her accounts in a much simpler form than the foregoing. The list of headings given above have been evolved to fit the life of a woman who has been at work for a number of years. A girl's first accounts may be as follows: Board and lodging; clothing; recreation and holidays; dentist and doctor; church and charity; savings; miscellaneous.

Mrs. Ellen Richards, whose work in teaching people how to live wisely is making her name more famous every year, gives in one of her books a division of a family income which every girl should study and try to understand: Food; clothes; rent or housing; light, heat and wages (operating expenses for the house); miscellaneous, including books, education, church, charity, savings, life insurance, doctor, dentist, travel and pleasure. Various divisions by percentages have been made of the family income. The one chosen by Mrs. Richards is based on an income of $1,000 a year. The percentages are 30 per cent. for food; 20 per cent. for rent; 15 per cent. for clothing; 10 per cent. for operating expenses; and 25 per cent. for miscellaneous.

It will be seen that there is a great deal for a girl to learn about the spending of money. She will readily understand that it is impossible for her to use her wages or income to the best advantage unless she knows what she is spending it for, and in what proportions. Every girl should make a division of income fitted to her own needs.

It is not always possible to follow the percentages which Mrs. Richards recommends, but it is possible and wise for every girl to know what are regarded as proper divisions for a family income, and to plan her own expenditures with such percentages as a guide.

Sometimes girls are called "fortunate" or "lucky" because their affairs seem to turn out well. In reality, these girls have planned carefully and have carried out their plans faithfully. A well managed life is not an accident, or a piece of luck; it is the result of careful planning, and persistent application.

The girl who saves has a freedom of action unknown to the girl who has never had a bank account. We all find a compelling necessity to spend money for food, shelter, clothing, carfare and other incidentals. But when these wants are satisfied, the wise girl puts by a certain part of her income. Then she can begin to exercise a power of choice. She may take some training which will help her to get a better position, she may learn a new occupation, or she may study music or designing. Possibly she needs a rest and change; if she has money saved, she may rest for a few weeks. If she has spent all her money, she must continue at work. Then, too, she should guard herself by the possession of a bank account against sickness, and being out of work. Even a small sum saved every week enables a girl to feel strong and self-reliant. The habit of saving calls for self-control, far-sightedness and imagination.

Girls invest their savings in various ways. A girl may help her people to buy a house, sometimes with a garden attached. This is a good investment in most circumstances. The girl should take an interest in the garden and help to grow vegetables and flowers. Possibly the garden lot may be large enough for poultry as well as vegetables. Or the girl's family may live outside the city, in which case a good part of the food for the household may be produced in the garden. It was one of the glories of Belgium before the war that many of her wage-earners lived in the country and grew a good part of their own food. They kept hens and pigs; and there was almost no unemployment or destitution in Belgium.

The girl who saves generally begins with a bank account and should learn to understand banking. The Canadian Government has an advantageous system of annuities which offers young investors an excellent return for them money. Girls and boys alike should study these annuities. Life insurance is a helpful form of investment for those who have dependents. The girl at work should not put her savings into speculative investments. Business men of the best standing say it is pathetic to see the waste of girls' savings in unwise investments. One of the best investments a girl can make is to continue her education.

CHAPTER XXV

HEALTH

Health has more to do with our successful employment than most of us have yet realized. To prove that this is true a woman who is an employment expert told the following story:

"The other night I was sitting in my office waiting for a girl who could not come to see me in the daytime. The manager of a business house who was interested in the girl had asked me if I would advise her how to change her work from one employment which she liked fairly well to another in which she was greatly interested. I had formed no particular idea of what the girl would be like. My day had been full and I had had no time to consider her case, knowing only that she wanted to change her work, and that she was a girl who was already earning her living.

"She came in, looked at me with a straight, steady glance and offered me her hand with a simplicity which took no note of the fact that an older person is supposed usually to make the first advance. The fact that we shook hands gave me an opportunity to notice that her hand was neither nervous nor tremulous. The quality of her handclasp can be summed up in saying that it was reassuring and agreeable. I wonder if most people know how all these points are noticed by employment experts and employers. The way in which the girl looked at me and the way in which she shook hands told me that she was physically and mentally in good condition.

"She was about five feet ten, and unusually well built and well developed. She was dressed in noticeably good taste. She was a rather large woman, or rather girl, for she was only a child in years. She was not what anyone would call 'a beauty,' but she was so splendidly well and carried herself so finely that she made an excellent impression. I do not know when I have been so much attracted by anyone. Almost any employer would have given her a position if he had had one vacant which she could fill. I wish all girls could realize what an advantage it is to be well physically and mentally and to look as well as this girl did.

"When I came to question her I found that her story was unusual from the point of view of employment. I thought from her appearance that she might be eighteen or nineteen. But to my astonishment she told me that she was fifteen and that she had been earning her living for nearly a year. She was a stenographer and had had three years' training in a high school of commerce. Her father had died and she was helping to support her mother. Several factors were against her satisfactory employment. She was under age and she had not completed her school course when she went to work. From these two facts it would have been natural to suppose that she would obtain a poor position, both in the character of the work required and in payment. She was earning fifteen dollars a week, a rate of payment three or four dollars a week higher than the average wage paid beginners in the city where she was employed. It was her splendid health, her look of substantial character and her good manner which had won this girl employment when another girl of fifteen, less healthy and less developed, might have failed to find any satisfactory position at all."

A time is likely to come in the world's history when the laws of right living are so well understood that poor health will be regarded as blameworthy. In a number of cases we must regard it as blameworthy now. To be in the company of a radiantly healthy person is a cheerful blessing. Let us make up our minds to be this kind of blessing to our friends.

Happily we can do a great deal to make ourselves healthy. We need to eat wisely, to dress properly and to rest well. Every girl should learn to regulate these things wisely for herself. Other people can only help to make us healthy, but the real work of being healthy we must do for ourselves, and this means daily attention and daily care. A famous doctor said once that the average baby is meant to live; all the baby asks is to be given a good chance. In the same way the average human being is meant to be healthy. Health depends — the statement is so important that it will bear repeating — on care in eating and resting and on proper clothing. Health depends also on cleanliness, inside the body and out; this means cleanliness in every respect. A daily bath and proper attention to one's body are essential to health.

The girl should learn as soon as possible that her health as well as her appearance will depend on her taking daily exercise. She may suppose that exercise is a dull tiresome thing which she is told by other people to take, but which in itself has no interest for her. Here, as in other things, the girl must learn to be her own captain, her own commanding officer. She should give herself orders to take daily exercise. If any of us needs a lesson in keeping well and beautiful, we can get that lesson from our little friends the birds. Every creature, wild and tame, winged and four-footed, takes the most scrupulous care of its physical condition. They clean, stretch, brush, polish, until every feather or hair, until every muscle and sinew is in fit condition.

We should think of our bodies as fine instruments which are given into our keeping. The human body is the finest and most wonderful instrument in the world, and it is sad and amazing how often we fail to take the most ordinary care of it. There are different systems of exercise, and the girl should find one that will bring all her muscles properly into play. Five or ten minutes' exercise a day is all that is required. There are many muscles which are not used in walking or ordinary play, and if these muscles are not exercised regularly then that fine instrument your body will get out of good condition and will not show correct and beautiful lines. A girl should train herself to stand properly. A simple test by which she can tell if she is holding herself rightly is to walk a few steps on tiptoe. In order to do this she must hold herself correctly. To have a good body, well shaped and in right proportion, it is necessary to hold one's self correctly all the time. Habits such as these are not acquired all at once. It is only by persistence day by day that the girl will learn to walk and to stand properly and will find that her body is becoming lithe, strong and healthy, an instrument which it is a joy to use and which will make her appearance as attractive as it ought to be.

When anything goes wrong which we do not understand, it is generally necessary to consult a physician. Special care should be taken to see a good doctor or dentist, if anything is wrong with eyes or teeth.

Other aids to health and happiness are sunshine and fresh air, drinking plenty of good water, useful work, good temper, and good times. To be healthy and happy we must also give affection and kind help to other people.

Like everyone else, the girl at work needs holidays. Two weeks in the year is a usual allowance; but three weeks are better than two. After the girl has become a responsible and important worker, she will find two holidays in the year a good investment for health, a short holiday and a longer one of three or four weeks.

To be angry, bad tempered and to think unkindly are all harmful to one's health and destroy a great part of one's happiness. No one can be a successful worker of a high type who is habitually jealous or bad-tempered. Good thoughts are an aid to both health and happiness. In the same way one needs what are called "good times." Many girls love walks in the country with a number of companions. Learning to know birds and flowers by sight, and keeping a record of those found, and when and where they were found, is an enjoyable pursuit of endless interest. Learn to keep and cherish all the festivals of the year—Christmas, New Year's, Thanksgiving, and other holidays. Charades and plays, games and dancing, picnics and excursions, may be made enjoyable and delightful and should help to keep girls healthy as well as happy if they are planned with good sense and restricted to suitable times and places.

CHAPTER XXVI

A GIRL'S READING

Anyone who has developed a love for reading possesses resources for self-improvement and enjoyment which are almost limitless. This love for reading a girl may acquire when she is young, or she may develop it at any time. It is worth while taking some trouble to learn to read well.

Reading for the girl at work should include newspapers and magazines as well as books. She should learn how to read newspapers, because as a great journalist said once, "A newspaper is a sign post telling the traveller which road he ought to take." In this sense we are all travellers and every worker needs to read his sign post which is a newspaper. To each girl some parts of a newspaper are more important than others; much depends on her occupation and on her relations to life. The business man reads the newspaper to find out what is happening that will affect his business. The girl at work should read what we call foreign news, that is, news about countries other than our own, and she should read also about important happenings in our own country. We ought to read the newspaper carefully so that we may be in touch with the rest of the world. We should read important local news, that is, news of our own neighbourhood. We cannot understand our neighbourhood unless we know what is going on in it. A new library may have been opened, a new church or picture gallery. Some worth while person may be speaking whom we may go to hear. There may be trouble in the community which we can help to put right. The person who is really living in touch with progress must give some time to daily newspapers.

But there is a good deal in a newspaper which one does not need to read. A newspaper is a report of daily happenings, sometimes even of rumours. These should be published, so that the truth may be arrived at, but the girl at work should find the parts of the newspaper which are her special concern and should not give much time to the rest of the paper. She should learn to distinguish facts from rumours and opinions. The girl who is learning discrimination in buying will find some of the advertisements useful reading.

Magazines are more like books than newspapers. Sometimes they are not so useful as newspapers. But they are often entertaining, and good entertainment is a fine thing. There are magazines which make a special feature of publishing articles on what is new in art, science, music, politics, etc. A number of good magazines are devoted especially to the interests ofwomen. The girl should not attempt to buy many magazines. A great many of them are alike. She should find one that meets her needs, and sometimes she should vary her choice.

It is important that she should see some of the best publications which have to do with her own line of work. If the girl is working at home she should read about home questions. Admirable new publications are being issued on all kinds of household matters. If a girl is a saleswoman or stenographer, she should see what is being written on these subjects. It is a mistake for any worker not to make herself familiar with what other workers in her own occupation are doing.

Besides reading for our work, we have minds and souls to keep and cultivate. Reading of the right kind is a great help in encouraging the growth of mind and soul. Books, when they are good of their kind, and when read in the right way, teach us; give us rest, change and variety; entertain and amuse us; and are a refuge and consolation.

We can learn a great deal from a good book of fiction. One writer has said that she obtained the greater part of her education from reading novels. Stories explain to us the endless varieties of human nature. We learn to know people from reading good novels, and after a while we are able to criticize the characters in the stories from the people we know ourselves. Then we can tell whether the novel is true to nature, or whether it is only a poor mistaken interpretation of life. Many novels have to do with famous places as well as famous people. It would be a great loss if we had to give up all the good novels in the world. The best novels help us to understand how wonderfully important life is.

Other realms of knowledge and delight are found in biography and history. Scarcely too much can be said in praise of good biography. The girl should ask at home or in a library for an interesting life of some famous person. Perhaps she is specially attracted to a hero or heroine of history, to some famous writer, artist or musician. In any case, she may ask the librarian to advise her which biography to read first. While reading famous histories, such as Greene's Short History of England, she should not fail to read the history connected with her own neighbourhood. World history and the history of countries other than our own are also important.

Besides fiction, biography and history, the girl is likely to find herself longing to read some of the great poetry of the world. Here again she may ask the advice of the librarian. We can hardly know the full beauty of God's world until we have read some of the writings of the great poets. The girl who is really fond of reading will enjoy essays and the letters of famous people. Girls who love art and music will find good books on such subjects. Almost anything one can imagine has been written about in a book.

While she should read well and wisely, the girl should not turn into a bookworm. Unless our reading fits us for better thought and better action, we should examine into what we are reading and change it for something better. Reading should never be a hindrance to work, but a help. Nor should we put reading in the place of people. It is a poor plan for any girl to prefer books habitually to intercourse with her friends.

A number of fine books deal with social and economic questions. These subjects appear also in many novels. The girl who wants to see conditions improved for the sick, the poor, and the unfortunate may again ask advice from the librarian. The biography of a woman like Miss Nightingale, or such a book as Ruskin's "Sesame and Lilies," will interest girls of this class.

A few rules will help us in our reading. Whatever book we read should be a good book of its class. Suppose we want to read a light and entertaining book for amusement and relaxation, then it should be good entertainment, well written, well planned, delightfully easy and gay in style. Do not read books which make you wish that you had not read them. Shun books which make one feel that life is not worth living. We can always judge the character of a book by the importance it gives to life. A book that has a great vision of life is a great book. In the same way we should not read books that make us think poorly of people. The finer the book the more clearly it shows how worth while every individual is. Any book that separates us, or turns us away, from the highest, happiest things is not worth the time which we might spend in reading it. There is something wrong with a book which leaves us indolent and listless. Books that we should choose, therefore, are those which make us feel that life is worth living, that people are worth while, and which keep us in love with the highest things in life.

CHAPTER XXVII

NECESSARY WORK

There is a question which everyone should ask herself about her work: "Is the work that I am doing adding anything to the wealth and well-being of the world? Is it necessary work—that is, is any one single person dependent to any extent for his or her existence on what I do?"

Necessary work has to do with providing the necessaries of life. These are food, clothing, shelter, light, heat and every other service or commodity which helps to keep us alive and adds to our efficiency as human beings.

Anyone, therefore, who is producing food or preparing it is a necessary worker. So are the great armies of workers who are engaged in producing materials out of which all kinds of necessary clothing are made, and other workers who make necessary clothing from wool, cotton, linen, etc.

Such workers occupy an honourable place because our lives actually depend on them. Their daily work adds to the wealth of the world and makes it possible to improve the standard of living for everyone. We could spend much time naming the occupations of necessary workers, such as fishermen, sailors, railway men, farmers, miners, and many others. Sailors and railway men are not directly engaged in creating new wealth as the farmer is, but food would not do us much good if there were no one to bring it to market, so all transportation workers are necessary workers.

Mothers of children add infinitely to the wealth and well-being of the world. Every girl or woman whose work it is to prepare food and make a home is a necessary worker of honourable rank. The paid house worker is a necessary worker and has this honourable rank.

Whether or not we are engaged in necessary work makes a great difference to the steadiness of our employment. If we are doing necessary work, we are much more certain of steady employment than we can be if our work is connected with providing luxuries or other commodities which are not essential to the maintenance of life.

About twice in every ten years, the world, or part of the world, experiences what is known as a financial depression. Perhaps crops have failed in many countries, or unwise people have been speculating madly, or a great amount of money has been invested in utilities which will not become productive for a number of years. Whatever the reason is, the world passes through a time of business depression. Every worker, young and old, should remember that these times of depression will recur. In good times when we are earning good wages we must prepare for these bad times when wages may be lower, or we may be out of work altogether and have no wages for some months. If we are not primary producers, such as the people in the classes named above, then it is wise for us to learn how to do some necessary work so that when a business depression comes, if we lose our usual employment, we may turn to this other vocation which we have learned.

Some girls earn wages by curling feathers. Now feathers are a luxury. No one needs to wear a feather in her hat in order to keep alive. But we know that we must eat, be clothed and have shelter in order to live. In times of great business depression people stop spending money, as far as possible. They cease buying feathers and other luxuries. In this way, girls who earn their living by doing work connected with luxuries are likely to lose their employment during times of financial depression. But if the girl who has earned her living curling feathers is a good cook, she is reasonably sure of employment even in bad times. Workers such as artists of all kinds, musicians, writers, actors, painters, sculptors, handicraft workers, architects and so on are likely to experience difficulties during times of financial depression. Many workers in these classes agree that it is advisable for them to have other work of a different character which they may use as occasion requires.

The girl who is a musician may add to her profession a knowledge of poultry farming or rose growing. Roses may be called a luxury, it is true, but the world will never consent to live without roses. Or the girl who is an artist may make and sell blouses. The girl who is a writer may find productive work of the same character as the musician, or she may turn to fruit farming or become a paid housekeeper. Every worker should make an effort to understand the connection between the character of her work and the likelihood of her obtaining steady employment.

CHAPTER XXVIII

WHAT ONE GIRL CAN DO FOR ANOTHER

"No work will have as much happiness as it ought to have, or will be as well done as it should be, until fellow-workers exchange experiences and advice with one another."

Every girl can learn something about her work from others in the same occupation. To learn from a friendly fellow-worker is pleasant and easy compared with the difficulty that we find in learning from people who are not specially interested in showing us how to work. Some of the happiest groups of workers are those who have organized to promote friendship and good feeling amongst girls and women who are in the same occupation.

This is what the girls of one such group say of the benefit of belonging to a friendly social organization of which the members are fellow-workers: "It improves our work, because we know how the others do theirs and we want to do as well as they do. We talk over problems in our work, and hearing the various ideas and solutions that others have thought out helps us in solving our problems. We do not meet to discuss our work primarily; as a rule our gatherings are for enjoyment and recreation. But work every now and then comes into general conversation and in this way we learn. It is a help to have for a friend one of the best workers in your occupation. You try your best to keep up with her. If any of the girls needs a new position, or is in difficulty about her work, she may talk it over with one of the older workers. In the same way we advise one another about wages. We can find out what is the average wage and the best wage paid in the occupation and what are the average hours of employment. Many girls in the club have found new positions and have been able to ask for and get higher wages through the advice and help of other club members."

Every girl knows what a help it is to work with others when sewing, mending, dressmaking and trimming hats. The girl in paid employment finds this work more trying than the girl who remains at home, because the girl at home generally has spare hours during the day when she may do work of this character. A mending circle meeting once a week could plan some entertainment to accompany work. One of the circle might read aloud, or all the members might take turns in telling a story and adding in some way to the evening's entertainment. Girls in such a circle could all help in blouse making or in millinery. One or more of the members might have a special gift in cutting and fitting. Others might be more skilful in sewing. One or more of the girls might have a special gift in buying. The possibilities of co-operative work of this kind for girls in the twentieth century are very great indeed.

There was a time in the history of the world when work of this kind was all done in private homes. Women and girls worked together at home, spinning, weaving, sewing and dressmaking. A great part of such work is now done in factories. But girls know that they still have mending, sewing, dressmaking and millinery to do. People are seldom well advised if they do work of this kind in isolation. The work is often not so well done and the worker is lonely and apt to be discouraged. It is part of the duty of the twentieth century girl to restore happiness and companionship in all this women's work, a great part of which is still done by hand. The happy circle of girl workers is often the best solution to the problem of how this work of making, trimming and mending should be done.

One such group of girls, in this case, a group of stenographers, who, as it happens, have all come from farm homes, have made a success of co-operative housekeeping. There are eight girls in the group. The city in which they work is by a lake and during the summer months these girls rent a cottage on the lake shore outside the city. They have the cottage for four months. Two girls undertake the housekeeping for a month at a time, which means that each girl has one month of housekeeping responsibility and three months when she helps only with tidying and cleaning. Their individual expenses for rent and housekeeping amount to $4.50 per week. This is an excellent example of the good to be obtained from co-operative effort.

Other girls find companionship, recreation and improvement in reading circles, study clubs, and clubs for walking, snowshoeing, skating and other outdoor enjoyment. Clubs formed to promote play and exercise are among the best of these organizations. Some circles are for dancing; others are dramatic clubs. Practically every group of this kind undertakes some benevolent work, and should do so in order to share happiness and good times with others. Such clubs entertain the inmates of hospitals, children's and old people's homes, give Christmas trees to children, send gifts to the needy, or work for benevolent organizations.

The club for outdoor play is one of the most important of group organizations. It has a wonderful effect on the health of its members. Tennis, basket ball, cricket, hockey and croquet are played by groups of girls who often challenge boys' clubs and are able to enter such contests with skill and ability. The gardening club is one of the many ways in which a club of girls can raise money to help in benevolent and other objects.

To form a group of this kind successfully the girl members require to have kindly impulses and enthusiasm, a willingness to work and play together, and the wish to be useful and to do something worth doing. Other requisites are a few simple rules, loyally lived up to, and one or two girls who have organizing ability. Leaders should train others to lead also, and each girl should take her turn in leading and in following.

The ideal group is not made up of girls exclusively, but should take its pattern as much as possible from family life. The girls of the group play together and work together. But the fathers and mothers of some of the girls will be glad to be honorary members and should share at times both in work and in play. A boys' club may be a friendly rival in games and may co-operate in benevolent work and entertainment.

CHAPTER XXIX

CIVIC DUTIES AND RESPONSIBILITIES

Learning to be a good neighbour is an active enjoyment which lasts us all our lives. Our civic duties and responsibilities may be summed up by saying that they are the duties and opportunities of a good neighbour. We should study our civic duties and responsibilities carefully so that we may know how to vote rightly and wisely when we are given an opportunity to vote on public questions.

The privilege of voting as a citizen is of the highest importance. But it is not by any means the only duty or opportunity of a good neighbour. Women have exercised the right to vote only of recent years, and still in a number of countries women do not yet vote.

They can and do give service in many other ways. Every man and woman who has the franchise should record an honest and intelligent vote. But those who vote should give other service as well. Those who are too young to vote have other opportunities to work for the community and for the nation.

The right to vote in Canadian elections for the Dominion House of Commons was given to a limited number of women for the first time in 1917. By an Act of Parliament which became law in 1918 all women in Canada have the right to vote in Dominion elections under the same conditions as men. Women of twenty-one and over have the right to vote in the Provincial elections of Ontario, British Columbia, Alberta, Saskatchewan, Manitoba, and Nova Scotia.

What is the meaning of learning to be a good neighbour?

Let us take the cases of three Canadian girls. One lives in a country neighbourhood, one belongs to a village, and the third is a city girl. Each of them lives in a house on a road or street. Other houses in which neighbours live are not far away. The city girl's next door neighbour is close by; there is more space in the village; and where the country girl lives everyone owns a farm so that there is abundance of room between one neighbour and another.

The community in which she lives gives each of these girls certain good things. It gives her the school where she is educated. The roads that lead to different places where she needs to go are provided by the community.

When a great many people live close together, the community has to provide other necessary things. The girl in the country neighbourhood, unlike the city girl, needs no special playground because she has many beautiful, safe places where she can play; also her father can provide his house with pure water with comparative ease, whereas in a city or town, the council, which is the government of the local community, provides water and playgrounds. The city girl is used to having these things provided for her by the community, and the girl in the country often does not stop to think of the space, light, air and water which are hers so freely and abundantly.

What we call the community is all the people who live in one district, which has boundaries to mark it off from other communities. Certain utilities, such as roads, schools, courts, water, lighting, parks, playgrounds, and many other things, are kept up by taxes, which are paid by the people of the community.

Sometimes taxes are objected to as burdens. But it is honourable to pay taxes for the upkeep of a good community. Money raised by taxes should be spent wisely, honestly, and not extravagantly. It is the people's money, and proper value should be received for what the community spends. We should all see as far as possible that the money from taxes is spent properly.

Every girl, boy, man and woman, is a citizen of some community and nation, and has a duty to see that the community and nation are well managed and well governed.

There is a beautiful word, common, which is sometimes misused in one of its meanings. One of the meanings of the word "common" is "belonging to all." Common property means property belonging to a certain number of people. A "common" is a piece of public property. A common duty is a duty which belongs to all. There is no common or public property in your neighbourhood, and there is no common duty in your neighbourhood, which is not yours.

To be a good neighbour has both a public and a private meaning. You are a good neighbour to the people who live near you if you help to take care of them when they are sick, do everything you can to keep them healthy when they are well, and are kind when they are in trouble. A good neighbour is a quiet, peaceful, law-abiding citizen, pleasant and useful in the neighbourhood. What you do as a good neighbour for the people who live next door, you do as far as you are able for the community in which you live. The best rule ever given to the world for being a good neighbour is contained in the story of the Good Samaritan. The more we study that story, the better we will understand our duties to our neighbours and the community.

Women and girls should be specially interested in such questions as education and the training of children, in public health and safety and public justice, in markets and everything having to do with the food supply, and in the proper treatment of immigrants. The nation cannot do its best unless girls and women help by being good neighbours and citizens in all these and other matters.

Perhaps the most valuable possession that any girl has is her character. The honest, kind, likeable girl, who keeps her word and is a good friend, is valued by everyone who knows her. The character of a nation is not unlike the character of the individual. We love our country. We would give her the best service. The best we can do for her is to make her national character honest, kind, strong, helpful and lovable. Every individual in a nation has a civic duty and responsibility to make that nation a good neighbour.

A Canadian woman of seventy years said once to a younger woman who was a professional worker, "My dear, tell me about the hospital where you are working. I have heard that conditions are not all they should be. I want to know, because if I know I may be able to help in making what is wrong right." She was a quiet, gentle woman, charming in manner, and somewhat shy and reserved. She never talked about disagreeable things. On this occasion she believed it was her duty to make sure whether there was a wrong, and if there was to try to put it right. No one ever heard anything said about this matter in public, but after some time the management of one public institution was greatly improved. Age, experience and wisdom can help in these wonderful ways. Girls may learn from such women.

We learn best to be good citizens in our own homes. Study public affairs and community questions with your father and mother, brothers and sisters.

Those who read Queen Victoria's Letters, which have been published, notice that in her girlhood she was a simple, gentle, innocent girl, not specially clever, but eager to learn, resolved that everything in the government of her country should be explained to her so that she might understand it. It was her duty to know the details of that great government, and she was determined, no matter what it cost her in work and study, to know and understand her duty. In her later letters she appears as an old, very wise woman, one of the first statesmen of her age. Queen Victoria had great responsibilities. Ours are smaller. But no girl, whether she works at home or in paid employment, can reach her highest development in the twentieth century without living up to her civic and national responsibilities.

CHAPTER XXX

THE BEST KIND OF WORK

Summing up what we have been able to learn, and what the world has learned, about employment, it is generally agreed that hard work is best. By hard work is meant work which requires from us the putting forth of all our energies and which calls for all our gifts. Work is very beneficial. As a man has said, "It takes the nonsense out of people," not the fun out of life, but the nonsense out of people, foolish, wrong, mistaken ideas which make people disagreeable to work with or play with or live with. It is not until our work, and methods of doing work, make use of all our ability and capacity that we know how fine work can be. You remember the story in the Bible which tells how Jacob wrestled with an unseen adversary until the breaking of the day. Then when Jacob was asked what he would have, he answered, "I will not let thee go except thou bless me." So work when we do our best with it blesses us.

Musicians speak of "technic" in playing and artists of "technic" in painting. Technic is skill, but it is more than skill. It is skill and individuality joined together. There is technic of a certain kind which we all may acquire in our work. Perhaps a story will explain best what this technic is. A beautiful girl who had all the gifts of a great actress but was untrained once made an extraordinary success in one of Shakespeare's plays. Later she failed utterly. She had not had that patient unceasing practice which makes every performance a high level of acting. When she felt inspired, she could act; but when she was dull or tired or out of sorts, her inspiration failed her, and she had no technic or skill in acting to fall back upon.

The good cook practically never fails in what she makes. She may not feel like cooking her best every day, but she knows how, and all her good work in the past stands by her skilful hands and makes her cooking a success every day. In the same way, the practised writer can rely on a certain technic or skill in writing even when he is dull and jaded and yet there is work which must be done.

In your work, no matter what it is, do your best every day as far as you are able, and by and by this skill in work will stand beside you like a friend and will help your hands and mind.

Have you ever noticed how a mother who has brought up five or six children of her own, takes a baby up in her hands? Such skill in handling an infant is one of the most beautiful things in the world. The mother can do it well, because she has done it often, with all her heart.

We often hear of success and failure in work. Good work is made up of both failure and success. One failure may spur us on to do better work than we have ever done before. A failure may teach us a great deal if we will learn from it. Do not be cast down because of failure. Find out what its lesson is. Do not be too much uplifted over a success. It may turn out a hindrance if we grow conceited over it. Both success and failure are temporary phases of good work.

We should learn not to try too hard, or be over anxious about work. Once an old gentleman who had taken up golf late in life said that his caddy had taught him a great lesson. "You are too anxious." the little boy said. "Just do as well as you can and don't be so anxious. You would play a better game that way."

We do not always believe when we are learning that work will be enjoyable. We have to learn *how to work* before we can get the full enjoyment from our occupation. You had to learn how to skate and how to dance before you enjoyed skating and dancing. Trying to skate and trying to dance and being awkward, and not knowing how, does not give one the full enjoyment of skating and dancing. But when we do know how and have become skilful, how delightful these recreations are! When we know how to work, work also is full of enjoyment.

It is well to remember that work is a permanent part of our lives. Do not think of it, therefore, as a harsh or unfriendly part of life, but realize the meaning of employment as one of our greatest possessions. It is a means by which we can enter into the full enjoyment of our own faculties and which helps us to understand the importance of life. The comradeship of work is very real and lasting. The girl who goes forward, therefore, into her life's work with a determination to do her best, while she will often meet hard problems, is certain to find usefulness and happiness in her employment.

FOOTNOTES:

[1] Acknowledgment is made to Miss B. L. Hutchins' *Women in Modern Industry*. G. Bell & Sons

.

[2] To write down even the names of the industries which are carried on in factories with the help of girls and women would occupy much space. A few of the more important places of industry in which girls are employed are whitewear factories and other factories which have to do with the making of clothes, factories where food is prepared for household use, twine factories, paper-box establishments, cigar and tobacco factories, bookbinding establishments, brush-making factories, manufactories of leather, carpets and rugs, boots and shoes and buttons, cotton and woolen-mills, and knitting mills. These are only a few of the factory employments, but the list shows how necessary the work of girls and women is to the nation's industry.

LIST OF OCCUPATIONS

Accompanying, see music.

Accounting.

Acting.

Advertising.

Anaesthetist.

Architecture.

Auditing.

Banking.

Basketry.

Bee-keeping.

Blouse making.

Bookbinding.

Bookkeeping.

Business managing and owning.

Butter making.

Buying, see store employment.

Candy making.

Canning.

Care of children.

Catering.

Cheese making.

Chemical industry.

Children's clothes making.

Children's nurse.

China decorating.

Chiropody.

Civil service.

Commercial traveller.

Companion.

Composition, see music.

Comptometer operating.

Concert singing and playing.

Confidential clerk.

Cooking.

Costume designing.

Dancing.

Deaconess.

Dentistry.

Designing fabrics, wall papers, etc.

Dictaphone operating.

Dietetics.

Domestic science:
Cook, special cooking, dietitian, manager of clubs, hotels, restaurants,
tea rooms and cafeterias, lecturer, teacher, writer.

Domestic service, see house employment.

Draughting.

Drawing.

Dressmaking:
Designing, sewing, buying, machine operating, managing and owning.

Embroidery.

Employment expert.

Enameling.

Entertainer.

Etching.

Expert in flour testing.

Factory employment:
Machine operators, designers, forewomen, stenographers, bookkeepers,
nurses, dietitians, welfare workers, travellers, managers and owners.

Farm work for women:
Farm managing, bee-keeping, plant growing, flower growing, poultry and
eggs, butter, milk and cheese, vegetables, fruit growing.

Farm managing.

Florist.

Flower growing.

Food demonstrating.

Fruit growing.

Governess.

Hairdressing.

Handicrafts:
Basketry, book binding, china decorating, embroidery, enameling, jewelry making, leather work, metal work, pottery, stencilling, weaving, wood carving.

Home making.

Hostess, in hotels, clubs, etc.

House decorating.

House furnishing.

House employment:
Cook, laundress, housemaid, children's nurse, seamstress, ladies' maid,
companion, mother's help, housekeeper, household manager and organizer.

Illustrating.

Instructor in wireless telegraphy.

Insurance.

Investigating, see social work.

Jewelry making.

Journalism.

Landscape architecture.

Landscape gardening.

Laundry.

Law.

Leather work.

Lecturing.

Library work.

Machine operating.

Manicuring.

Map making.

Massage.

Medicine.

Metal work.

Milk farming.

Millinery:
Making, designing, selling, managing, owning.

Missionary work.

Mother's help.

Motor driving.

Munitions.

Music:
Accompanying, composition, concert playing and singing, teaching.
Nursing:
Institutional, private, military, public health, schools,
superintendents of hospitals and training schools, managing and
owning private hospitals.
Office employment:
Stenographer, typist, bookkeeper, confidential clerk, secretary,
billing clerk, cheque clerk, fyling clerk, dictaphone operator,
comptometer operator, librarian, manager.

Painting.

Pharmacy.

Photography.

Police woman.

Postal clerk.

Pottery.

Poultry farming.

Proof reading.

Real estate:
Agents, rent collectors.

Salesmanship.

Sculpture.

Seamstress.

Secretarial work.

Sewing by the day, see seamstress.

Shampooing.

Shopping expert.

Social work:
Secretaries, statisticians, visitors, lecturers, dietitians, doctors, nurses, field workers, investigators, parole officers, officers of institutions, superintendents.

Statistical work.

Stencilling.

Stenography.

Store employment:
Messenger girls, parcel girls, markers, assistants, stenographers, shoppers, house furnishers, assistant managers, managers, assistant buyers, buyers, advertisers, nurses, dietitians, welfare workers, employment experts, owners.
Teaching:
Public schools, high schools, colleges, private schools, music, dramatic, domestic science, kindergarten, arts and handicrafts, lecturing, teaching handicapped children, manual training, sewing,

millinery, dressmaking, physical training, gardening, commercial
subjects, governess, tutor, secretary, supervising.
Telegraphy:
Morse operating, automatic machines.
Telephone employment:
Operating, supervising, private switchboard operating.

Vegetable growing.

Vocational advising.

Weaving.

Welfare work.

Window decorating.

Wood carving.

Work for the girl at home:
Blouse making, children's clothes, candy making, sewing, dressmaking,
millinery, bread making, cake and jam making, pickles, marmalade,
catering, shopping, embroidery, laundry work, mending, making
underclothes, canning, raising fruit and flowers, poultry and eggs,
vegetable growing, managing a lending library, teaching, mother's
help,
house work for neighbours, doctors' and dentists' secretary,
visiting bookkeeper, visiting housekeeper.

Writing.

BIBLIOGRAPHY.

Art of Right Living, The, by Ellen H. Richards: Whitcomb & Barrows, Boston (1904).

Business of Being a Woman, The, by Ida M. Tarbell: Macmillan,
New York, 1916.

Careers: Women's Employment Publishing Company, London,
1916.

Classified List of Vocations for Trained Women, by E. P. Hirth: The Intercollegiate Bureau of Occupations, New York, 1917.

Commercial Work and Training for Girls, by Jeannette Eaton and Bertha M. Stevens: Macmillan, New York, 1915.

Cost of Cleanness, The, by Ellen H. Richards: Wiley & Sons, New York (1908).

Cost of Food, The, by Ellen H. Richards: Wiley & Sons, New York (1901).

Cost of Living, The, by Ellen H. Richards: Wiley & Sons, New York (1899, 1905).

Cost of Shelter, The, by Ellen H. Richards: Wiley & Sons, New York (1905).

Democracy and Education, by John Dewey: Macmillan, New York (1916).

Domestic Needs of Farm Women. Report No. 104: U.S. Department of Agriculture, Washington, 1915.

Domestic Service, by C. V. Butler: G. Bell & Sons, London, 1916.

Economic Needs of Farm Women. Report No. 106: U.S. Department of Agriculture, Washington, 1915.

Economic Position of Women. Vol. I, No. 1. Proceedings of Academy of Political Science: Columbia University, New York, 1910.

Educational Needs of Farm Women. Report No. 105: U.S. Department of Agriculture, Washington, 1915.

Fatigue and Efficiency, by Josephine Goldmark: Charities Publication Committee, New York, 1912.

Food and Household Management, by Helen Kinne and Anna M. Cooley: Macmillan, New York, 1915.

Home and the Family, The, by Helen Kinne and Anna M. Cooley: Macmillan, New York, 1917.

Household Administration, edited by Alice Ravenhill and Catherine J. Schiff: Grant Richards, London, 1910.

Increasing Home Efficiency, by Martha Bensley Bruere and Robert W. Bruere: Macmillan, New York, 1913.

Industrial Democracy, by Sidney and Beatrice Webb: Longmans, Green, London, 1897.

Intercollegiate Bureau of Occupations, New York. Reports. 1911-1913, 1914-1915.

Life and Labour of the People of London, Vol. 4. Women's Work, by Charles Booth: Macmillan, London, 1902.

Life of Ellen H. Richards, by Caroline L. Hunt: Whitcomb & Barrows, Boston, 1916.

Living Wage of Women Workers, The, by L. M. Bosworth: Longmans, Green, New York, 1911.

Long Day, The: The Century Company, New York, 1905.

Making Both Ends Meet, by S. A. Clark and Edith Wyatt: Macmillan, New York, 1911.

Minimum Cost of Living, The, by Winifrid Stuart Gibbs: Macmillan, New York, 1917.

Minority Report of the Poor Law Commission, Part 2. The Unemployed.

New Era in Canada, The, edited by J. O. Miller: J. M. Dent & Son, London and Toronto, 1917.

Profitable Vocations for Girls, by E. W. Weaver: A. S. Barnes Company, New York, 1913.

Report of The Ontario Commission on Unemployment, 1916.

Road to Trained Service in the Household, The, by Henrietta Roelofs: National Board Young Women's Christian Associations, New York, 1915.

Saleswomen in Mercantile Stores, by E. B. Butler: Charities Publication Committee, New York, 1909.

Shelter and Clothing, by Helen Kinne and Anna M. Cooley: Macmillan, New York, 1915.

Social and Labour Needs of Farm Women, Report No. 103, U.S. Department of Agriculture, Washington, 1915.

Survey of Occupations Open to the Girl of Fourteen to Sixteen, by H.H. Dodge: Girls' Trade Education League, Boston, 1912.

Trade Union Woman, The, by Alice Henry: D. Appleton, New York, 1915.

Vocational Mathematics for Girls, by Wm. H. Dooley: D.C. Heath, Boston, 1917.

Vocations for Boston Girls. Bulletins. Telephone operating. Book-binding.
Stenography and typewriting. Nursery maid. Dressmaking. Millinery.
Straw hat making. Manicuring and hairdressing. Nursing. Salesmanship.
Clothing machine operating. Paper box making. Confectionery manufacture.
Knit Goods manufacture: Girls' Trade Education League, Boston, 1911, 1912.

Vocations for Girls, by Mary A. Laselle and Katherine E. Wiley: Houghton, Mifflin Company, Boston, 1913.

Vocations for the Trained Woman, Vol. 1, Pts. 1 and 2. Women's Educational and Industrial Union, Boston: Longmans, Green, New York, 1910, 1914.

Wage-Earning Women, by Annie Marion Maclean: Macmillan, New York, 1910.

Ways of Woman, The, by Ida M. Tarbell: Macmillan, New York, 1915.

Welfare Work, by Dorothea Proud: G. Bell & Sons, London, 1916.

Woman and Labour, by Olive Schreiner: T. Fisher Unwin, London, 1911.

Woman—Bless Her, The, by Marjory MacMurchy: S. B. Gundy, Toronto, 1916.

Women and the Trades, by E. B. Butler: Charities Publication Committee, New York, 1909.

Women and Work, by Helen M. Bennett: D. Appleton & Company, New York, 1917.

Women in Modern Industry, by B. L. Hutchins: G. Bell & Sons, London, 1915.

Women's Educational and Industrial Union, Boston. Reports, 1913, 1914.

Work-a-day Girl, The, by Clara E. Laughlin: Fleming H. Revell Company, New York, 1913.

Youth, School and Vocation, by Meyer Bloomfield: Houghton, Mifflin Company, Boston, 1915.